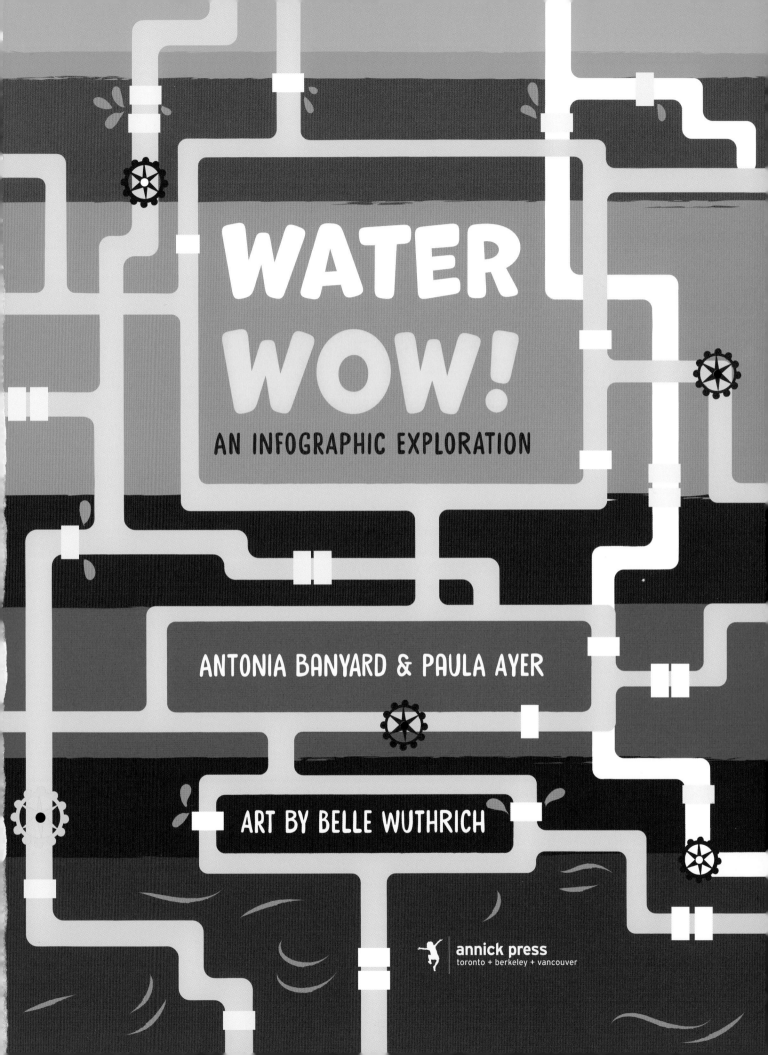

WATER WOW!
AN INFOGRAPHIC EXPLORATION

ANTONIA BANYARD & PAULA AYER

ART BY BELLE WUTHRICH

annick press
toronto + berkeley + vancouver

Proofread by Linda Pruessen
Designed by Belle Wuthrich

Annick Press Ltd.

We acknowledge the support of the Canada Council for the Arts, the Ontario Arts Council, and the participation of the Government of Canada/la participation du gouvernement du Canada for our publishing activities.

Cataloging in Publication

Banyard, Antonia, author

    Water wow! : an infographic exploration / Antonia Banyard and Paula Ayer ; illustrated by Belle Wuthrich.

Includes bibliographical references and index.
Issued in print and electronic formats.
ISBN 978-1-55451-821-0 (paperback).—ISBN 978-1-55451-822-7 (bound).—ISBN 978-1-55451-823-4 (html).—ISBN 978-1-55451-824-1 (pdf)

1. Water—Pictorial works—Juvenile literature. 2. Water—Juvenile literature. I. Ayer, Paula, author II. Wuthrich, Belle, 1989-, illustrator   III. Title.

GB662.3.B35 2016   j553.7   C2015-904559-2
                                   C2015-904560-6

Distributed in Canada by University of Toronto Press.
Published in the U.S.A. by Annick Press (U.S.) Ltd.

Distributed in the U.S.A. by Publishers Group West.

Printed in China

Visit us at: www.annickpress.com
Visit Belle Wuthrich at: bellewuthrich.com

Also available in e-book format.
Please visit www.annickpress.com/ebooks.html for more details. Or scan

CONTENTS

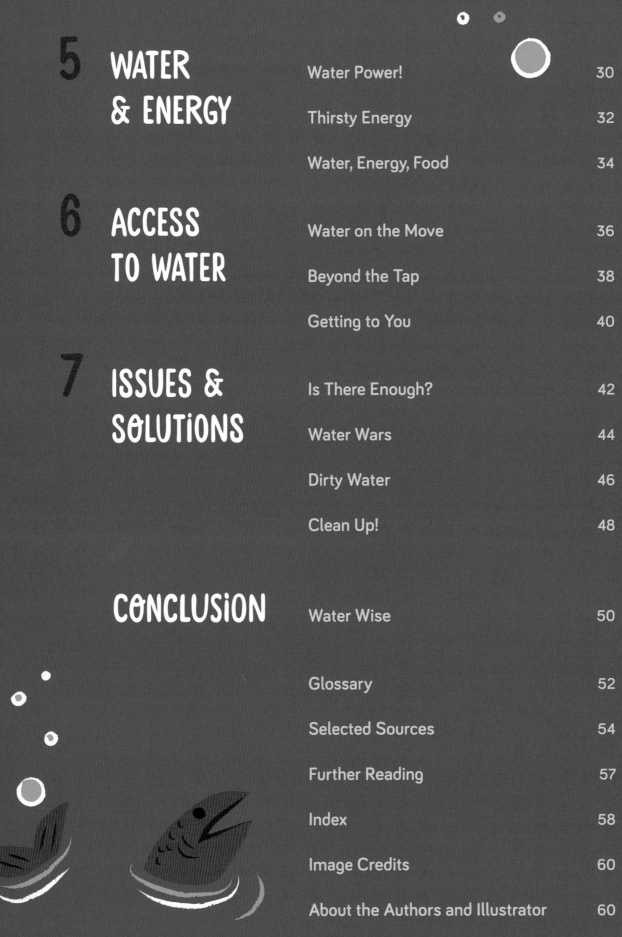

HOW TO READ THE WATER MEASUREMENTS IN THIS BOOK

IN THIS BOOK, we've used both metric and imperial measurements. But "20 liters of water" or "3 gallons" can be hard to picture. So sometimes, we've used everyday measurements like water bottles, milk jugs, or swimming pools to give a better idea of how much water we're talking about. Here's what we mean when we say …

1 cup = 250 milliliters (8 ounces), or the amount that would fit in a small glass

1 milk jug = 3.79 liters (1 gallon)

1 water cooler bottle = 19 liters (5 gallons), like the big bottles that go on top of water coolers

Bathtubs can hold varying amounts of water depending on their size and how much you fill the tub. When we say "a bathtub full," it means an average tub filled to the brim, or about 150 liters (40 gallons).

Showers can also vary depending on the water pressure of the showerhead. When we say "a five-minute shower," that means around 60 liters (15 gallons) of water.

An Olympic-sized swimming pool holds about 2.5 million liters (660,000 gallons) of water.

Sometimes, we need to measure really, really big quantities of water. How much? A LOT! For this, scientists and researchers use units called **cubic kilometers** and **cubic gigameters**. A cubic kilometer is an imaginary cube 1 kilometer (0.6 miles) on each side. That cube would hold over 984 billion liters (260 billion gallons), enough to cover the entire island of Manhattan in water 11.5 meters (37 feet) deep! But a cubic gigameter is *100,000 times bigger!* So one cubic gigameter would hold 98,400 trillion liters (26,000 trillion gallons)!

INTRODUCING THE AMAZING ... WATER!

IT FLOWS! IT FREEZES! It powers houses and buildings! It's in the air and in the ground. And even though you need it, you probably think of it only when there isn't any around. It's … water!

Care for a Glass of Dihydrogen Monoxide?

Relax—it's just water! That funny chemical name tells you what water's made of: two hydrogen atoms and one oxygen atom. (*Di* at the start of a word means "two" and *mono* means "one.") When those three atoms crash into each other hard enough, they stick together to make a water molecule.

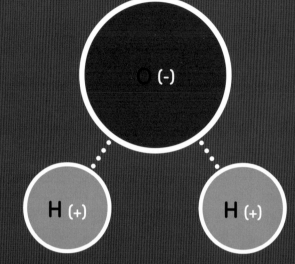

Cool Things About Water Molecules

THEY'RE CHARGED!

Think of a water molecule like a triangle with magnets at each point. The top point of the triangle (oxygen) has a negative charge, pulling it one way. The bottom two points (hydrogen) have a positive charge, pulling them in the opposite direction.

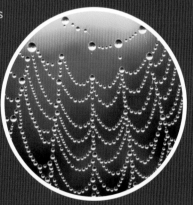

THEY LIKE TO STICK TOGETHER.

Water molecules are attracted to other water molecules because of that magnet-like charge. One molecule can pull as many as four other molecules around itself. Try dripping some water on a table. See how it forms rounded drops rather than flattening out? Now you know why!

THEY MOVE APART WHEN THEY COOL OFF.

Most things get smaller—or contract—when they get colder. Not water! Its molecules actually expand as they freeze, making frozen water less dense than the liquid form. That's why ice floats on top of water. This is a good thing for the fish that live at the bottom of lakes; otherwise they would become fishsicles.

Also Known As ...

You may have encountered H_2O in one of these forms:

ICE. Water's chilled-out solid form. Found in summer drinks, skating rinks, and hanging off the end of your nose in winter.

WATER. The good old liquid stuff, essential for drinking, bathing, and backyard water fights.

VAPOR. When water droplets get too hot, they like to dance around in the air and let off some steam. You'll encounter this gas form of water puffing out of kettles or rising over a hot bath.

Are There More Than Three States of Water?

Scientists say, yes! Water also exists under a mysterious alias called *supercritical fluid*, which acts a little bit like a gas and a little bit like a liquid. It tends to hang around in places you wouldn't exactly like to visit, such as vents at the bottom of the ocean or the inside of volcanoes.

Then there's another form so secret we can't even see it. *Hydrous minerals*—a fancy name for "watery rocks"—look like an average rock, but fused into the rock are molecules of water. This type of water is only found deep under the Earth's surface, where the intense pressure squishes the water molecules into the rock molecules. Amazingly, hydrous minerals are the most abundant source of water on Earth!

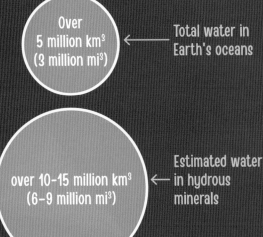

Over 5 million km³ (3 million mi³) ← Total water in Earth's oceans

over 10-15 million km³ (6-9 million mi³) ← Estimated water in hydrous minerals

It's Clear! No, it's Blue!

A glass of water is clear, right? So why do oceans, lakes, and swimming pools look blue? Sunlight or other white light contains all the colors of the rainbow. When light shines on water, the vibrating water molecules absorb all the colors of the rainbow except those at the blue end, which are reflected back to our eyes. Algae or other particles in the water and the reflection of the sky also make large bodies of water look blue. Even the pure water in your glass is a very light blue, but our eyes can only see it when light travels through deeper water.

WET PLANET

EARTH ISN'T CALLED THE BLUE PLANET for nothing. There's much more water on Earth than on any other planet in our solar system, and on most planets we know of in the universe. Without that water, Earth would be a boring rock with no plants, animals, or humans.

You probably already know about the water cycle: water falls as rain and evaporates back into the sky, over and over and over again. But have you ever thought about where all that water came from in the first place?

Cosmic Juice

Scientists believe that all water was formed in space, one molecule at a time, over billions of years, probably from hydrogen and oxygen that spewed out of exploding stars. Eventually, enough of these molecules found one another. First they formed a fine mist, then a droplet, and on and on.

How Old Is It?

Half of the Earth's water could have been formed in space even before the Sun existed—that's over *4.54 billion years ago!*

IN 1998, a team of scientists discovered a huge water factory in an interstellar gas cloud in the middle of Orion, a constellation in our solar system. This cloud of gas creates enough water to fill all of the Earth's oceans in less than half an hour. Every day, around the clock.

The Mystery of Water on Earth

Water from your tap might seem fresh and new. In fact, it's one of the oldest things on Earth! So how did it get here? Surprisingly, scientists aren't sure.

THEORY 1: IT CAME FROM OUTER SPACE!

The young Earth was a hot and atmosphere-less place, some scientists think, so it couldn't have held much water—it would have just boiled off or flown back into space. They say the water we have now was delivered by ice-carrying meteoroids or comets long after Earth was formed.

THEORY 2: IT WAS HERE ALL ALONG!

Other scientists say there's increasing evidence most of Earth's water was on the surface from the beginning. They believe that water was one of the raw space materials that crashed together to form the planet around 4.5 billion years ago.

THEORY 3: IT WAS JUST HIDING!

Still other theories suggest that water existed *in* the Earth, but didn't make its way to the surface until much later. It might have leaked out from hydrous minerals, or erupted out of volcanoes.

Where Else in the Solar System Is Water?

Our solar system isn't as dry as scientists used to think. Evidence of oceans has been found on several moons of Jupiter and Saturn, though the water is trapped under layers of rock and ice.

LIQUID WATER   ICE

POSSIBLE WATER   WATER VAPOR

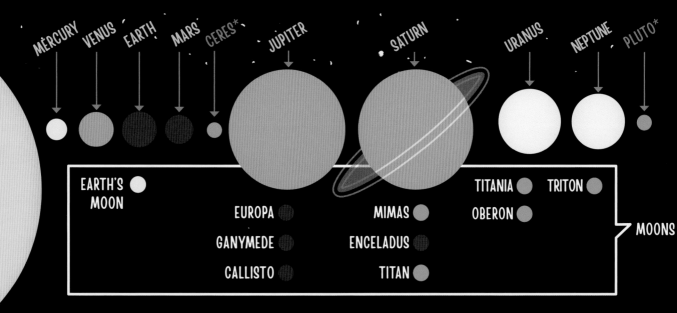

MERCURY   VENUS   EARTH!   MARS   CERES*   JUPITER   SATURN   URANUS   NEPTUNE   PLUTO*

EARTH'S MOON

EUROPA
GANYMEDE
CALLISTO

MIMAS
ENCELADUS
TITAN

TITANIA   TRITON
OBERON

MOONS

*Dwarf planet

WHERE ON EARTH IS THE WATER?

WHEN YOU LOOK AT A MAP, the world seems to be mostly water. But surprisingly, most of the planet is not water, and just a tiny part of the water that is here is fresh enough for us to use. So where *is* all the water? It might not be where you think!

If you were to roll out the surface of the Earth like a map, water would cover nearly three-quarters of it.

But if you could gather all of that water together into a ball, it would actually be only a tiny fraction of the Earth's mass—about 0.025%! That's because even though the oceans seem very deep, compared to the size of the Earth, they're spread in a thin layer—like the skin on an apple.

If the entire Earth were the size of your bedroom, all the water would fit in two milk jugs in the corner.

Where Can You Get a Drink around Here?

While the Earth may not have as much water as we're used to thinking it does, even that tiny blue dot on the globe still represents a lot of H_2O. But nearly all of that is salt water. Good for fish, but not for drinking!

3%
is freshwater

Only 3%? Well, there's more bad news: most of that small amount is frozen in glaciers and ice caps. Another big chunk is stored underground or in cracks in rock as groundwater.

68.7%
is in ice caps and glaciers

0.3%
is surface water
(freshwater that's above ground, like lakes and rivers)

97%
of water on Earth is in the oceans

31%
is groundwater
(water stored in the soil or in tiny holes in rock)

This tiny amount is the water we're most familiar with—what we use for drinking, watering our lawn, bathing, and everything else.

Where Can You Find Surface Water?

0.26%
IN LIVING THINGS

0.49%
RIVERS

2.6%
SWAMPS & MARSHES

69%
ICE IN THE GROUND & PERMAFROST

3.0%
ATMOSPHERE

3.8%
SOIL MOISTURE

20.9%
LAKES

Imagine if someone gave you $100, then took it all back except for three pennies. That's the difference between all the water on Earth and the surface water we can use!

EXTREME WATER

WATER IS ALWAYS AMAZING, but in some places it's worthy of the record books. Check out these hot spots (okay, more like wet and cold spots) around the globe.

WETTEST PLACE ON EARTH: *MT. WAIALEALE, HAWAII*

Which gets almost 12 m (38 ft) of rain in an average year

LONGEST RIVER: *THE NILE, NORTHEAST AFRICA*

LENGTH: 6,853 km (4,258 mi)—about the distance from Alaska to Florida

WHAT'S SO AMAZING? Though the Nile is the world's longest river, it used to be about 120% longer! It once flowed out of Lake Tanganyika, but around 12 million years ago it was blocked and shortened by newly formed volcanoes along the bottom of the Black Sea.

DRIEST PLACE ON EARTH: *IQUIQUE, CHILE*

Where there was no rain for 14 years!

LARGEST LAKE UNDER A GLACIER: *VOSTOK, ANTARCTICA*

AREA: 15,690 km² (6,060 mi²)—a bit larger than the state of Connecticut

WHAT'S SO AMAZING? The thick ice layer covering Lake Vostok has sealed off this underwater environment for about 15 million years. Lake Vostok might be on this planet, but scientists think it's probably a lot like the ice-covered ocean on Jupiter's moon Europa. The coldest temperature ever recorded was on Lake Vostok at a chilly -89.2°C (-128.6°F).

DEEPEST, COLDEST, AND WITH THE MOST WATER: *LAKE BAIKAL, RUSSIA*

MAXIMUM DEPTH: 1,637 m (5,371 ft)—two times the height of the Burj Khalifa, the world's tallest building

WATER VOLUME: 23,600 km^3 (5,700 mi^3)—enough to fill 9 billion Olympic-sized swimming pools!

WHAT'S SO AMAZING? About one-fifth of the world's unfrozen surface freshwater can be found here. Baikal is also the world's oldest lake; it's been around for 25 million years!

ONLY ACTIVE UNDERSEA RIVER: *BLACK SEA UNDERSEA RIVER*

FLOW: 22,000 m^3 (777,000 ft^3) of water per second

WHAT'S SO AMAZING? Discovered in 2010, this river would be the world's sixth-largest if it flowed above ground. Scientists have used a robotic submarine to study the salty waterway, which runs along the bottom of the Black Sea.

LARGEST TIDAL BORE: *QIANTANG RIVER, HANGZHOU, CHINA*

HEIGHT: 9 m (30 ft) —about three storeys tall

SPEED: as fast as 40 km (25 mi) per hour

WHAT'S SO AMAZING? A tidal bore is a strong tide that pushes up a river, against the current—a true tidal wave. Known as the "silver dragon," the tidal bore on the Qiantang River can be heard hours before it rushes up the river. Visitors can see the surge of water from tide-watching pavilions.

LARGEST PERMANENT DESERT LAKE AND LARGEST SALT LAKE: *TURKANA, ETHIOPIA AND KENYA*

AREA: 6,405 km^2 (2,473 mi^2) —the size of the state of Delaware

MAXIMUM DEPTH: 109 m (358 ft)—that's 10 utility poles stacked on top of each other

WATER VOLUME: 204 km^3 (49 mi^3)

WHAT'S SO AMAZING? This jade-colored lake isn't that big, but then again, it *is* in the desert and has an active volcano in the middle. Many anthropologists consider the wild and inaccessible area around Lake Turkana the birthplace of humankind because so many fossils of human ancestors have been found there.

WATER'S AMAZING JOURNEY

HOWEVER IT GOT TO EARTH, one thing is clear: there's no way to create new water on this planet. All the water we use is the same stuff that's been here for billions of years—going up into the sky and back down, over and over. That means the water in your glass has a long, long history. It might once have been dinosaur pee, or Cleopatra's bathwater, or rain that fell on your great-great-grandfather!

9 DAYS is how long an evaporated water molecule typically floats around in the sky before coming back to Earth as rain or snow.

2 MINUTES of evaporation off the world's oceans equals the amount of water Americans use in a day.

33% of water use in North America comes from groundwater. While a drop of water on the surface can go through the cycle of evaporation and rain over a few minutes, days, or weeks, water that sinks deep underground can stay there for thousands of years.

1 HOUR is the average lifespan of a cloud. Clouds form when evaporated water droplets gather together in the sky.

1 FOOTBALL FIELD of trees sends enough water into the air each day to fill a small backyard swimming pool. Trees and plants pull up water from the ground and "evapotranspire"— the plant version of sweating!— through their leaves.

2 MONTHS OF SHOWERS is what you could get from collecting all the water that falls on the roof of an average house during a moderate rainstorm.

AQUIFERS are layers of water-bearing rock, gravel, or sand under the ground. Aquifers can either be either *unconfined*, which means their water can flow up to the surface, or *confined*, which means the water is trapped underground.

EVAPORATION from groundwater can be absorbed by plants, even in deserts with no rain! Reflective blankets cover the ground and trap enough evaporated groundwater for seeds to sprout and grow.

WATER, WEATHER, AND CLIMATE

IF THE WEATHER were a (really long) movie, then water would be one of the lead actors. Weather is driven by the oceans, rain, and water vapor. And water is a key part of "extreme weather events"—otherwise known as floods, droughts, and storms.

How Does Water Affect Weather?

OCEAN WATER EVAPORATES and forms clouds, which are then pushed by winds over large distances before the water falls as rain. So even storms that happen far away from a coastline start in the ocean.

ICE AND SNOW COOL the Earth by reflecting the Sun's radiation. Glaciers store water and, when they melt in the summer, supply water throughout the dry months.

WHEN WATER EVAPORATES off the surface of the ocean, or any other body of water, it forms the atmosphere, which acts like a giant blanket around Earth and helps to hold in the Sun's warmth.

THE OCEANS absorb the Sun's heat and move it around the world in the form of ocean currents. Without these currents, the countries around the equator would be far too hot, and countries nearer the poles would be frigid.

Water Change = Climate Change

Water is also a major player in climate—the pattern of weather over time.
Scientists agree Earth's climate is changing, so what does that mean for water?

HEAVY RAINS can carry organisms that cause disease from the land into the water supply.

RISING TEMPERATURES will mean more evaporation.

MORE EVAPORATION will mean that some areas won't get enough rain while others will get more than they need.

MELTING GLACIERS and polar ice caps will mean more water in the oceans, so ocean levels will rise.

WARMER WINTERS will mean less snow and more rain. Because snow and ice act as water stores, this can lead to less water in the dry months, when we need it.

WARMER LAKE and ocean waters will affect sea plants and animals.

LESS WATER affects energy production, agriculture, human health, and the natural world.

MORE FLOODING will mean more sediment and runoff in our drinking water, which can overwhelm water filtration systems.

Climate change is already happening, but we can still put on the brakes. Everything you do to burn fewer fossil fuels, like oil and gas, helps. When possible, walk or bike instead of jumping in the car, shut off lights, and take shorter showers. If you can, shop less, reuse things, and try substituting meat and dairy with plant-based foods. Not only will you be helping keep the planet cool, but you'll contribute to healthy water, too!

DRY TIMES

DO YOU THINK of a desert or a dusty prairie when someone says *drought*? In fact, a drought just means less rain and snow than what's typical for an area. In a tropical rainforest, six days without rain could be considered a drought. In the dry Australian outback, it's perfectly normal to have months without rain.

Why So Dry?

Droughts can be caused by:

Not enough rain

A naturally occurring dry season

Irregular changes in weather patterns, such as El Niño—a period of warmer ocean currents

Human activities, like overfarming, too much irrigation, and deforestation

Climate change, which is predicted to cause more droughts in some areas and more floods in others

What Happens in a Drought?

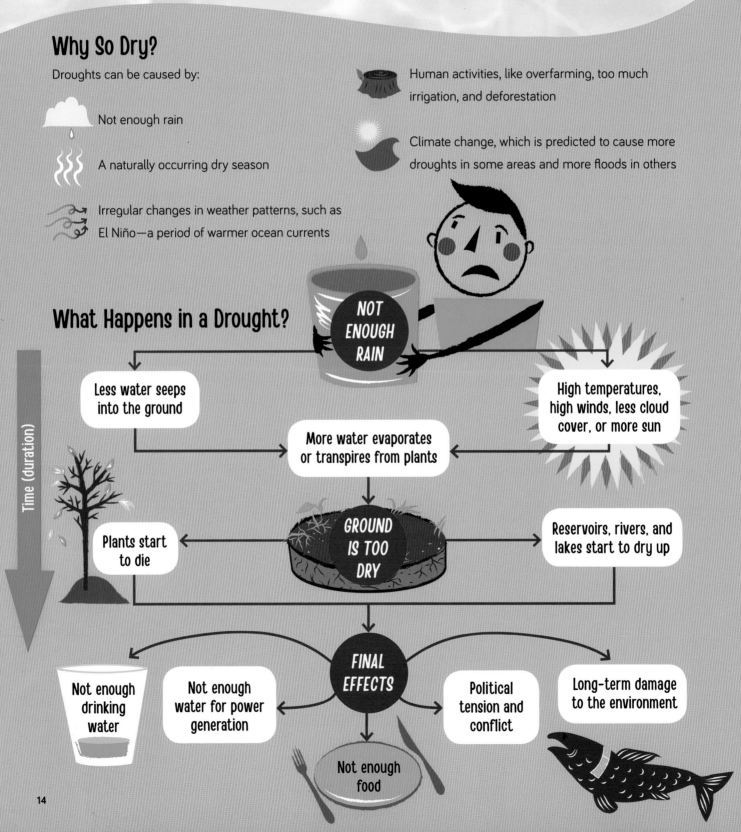

Time (duration)

NOT ENOUGH RAIN

Less water seeps into the ground

High temperatures, high winds, less cloud cover, or more sun

More water evaporates or transpires from plants

Plants start to die

GROUND IS TOO DRY

Reservoirs, rivers, and lakes start to dry up

FINAL EFFECTS

Not enough drinking water

Not enough water for power generation

Not enough food

Political tension and conflict

Long-term damage to the environment

A Dry History

Not only are droughts some of the earliest climate events ever recorded, but they're also a big reason for the movement of early peoples around the world.

7500 BCE, ATACAMA, CHILE

These salt flats in the Atacama Desert weren't always there. Around 13,000 BCE, the area was wet enough for people to live. But when a drought struck about 5,500 years later, humans quickly left.

1150–1200 CE, SOUTHWEST US

After about 400 years of on-and-off dry spells, a particularly bad drought finally forced the Ancestral Puebloans (also known as the Anasazi) to leave their communities. One famous site, Pueblo Bonito in Chaco Canyon, New Mexico, is shown here.

2200 BCE, AKKADIAN EMPIRE

This flourishing early empire in what is now Iraq was hit by a drought that lasted as long as 300 years. The Akkadians either starved or moved, and their empire collapsed.

1930s, THE DUST BOWL, US AND CANADA

A combination of three severe droughts and poor farming practices turned the once-productive North American prairie region into a desert. Winds blew loose dust across the landscape in huge clouds. Tens of thousands of families were forced to leave their farms to search for work during the Great Depression.

1780s–90s, FRANCE

The harsh winter of 1787–88, followed by a drought in the summer of 1789, fueled protests by the starving peasants of France, which led to the French Revolution.

2015, CALIFORNIA

In January 2015, California's governor declared a drought state of emergency and put strict limits on water use. Naturally changing weather patterns have had a bigger impact than usual because of global warming. Water shortages in California affect all of the US and Canada because so much food is grown there.

In Mozambique, long droughts mean residents often don't have clean water for drinking and growing food. But starting in 2006, communities in one area built dams and rooftop rain-collecting systems, which captured enough water in the rainy season to last all year.

THE SOUP OF LIFE

IT'S ALIVE! Okay, not exactly, but if you look at a drop of water from a natural source under a microscope, you'll discover a lot of life. Everything from tiny microorganisms to giant mammals make water their home, and even animals and plants that don't *live* in water need it to survive. When astronomers search for signs of life on other planets, the first thing they look for is— you guessed it—water. In *liquid* form. Why is that?

Liquid Assets

Liquid is essential for life because it allows molecules to dissolve and move around. That means life-supporting chemical reactions can happen—like digestion in animals and photosynthesis in plants. But why water and not some other liquid? Well, water stays liquid under many conditions. Most other substances are only liquid at extreme temperatures or pressures.

IMAGINE IF WATER only stayed liquid at half this range. Most of Earth's water would evaporate during the day and freeze solid at night or in winter. Life as we know it would be impossible!

Water's Liquid Range

SALTY WATER—like the stuff found in oceans—can get much colder than freshwater before it freezes.

-46°C (-50°F)	-0°C (32°F)	100°C (212°F)	340°C (650°F)
Freezing point (salt water)	Freezing point (freshwater)	Boiling point (sea level)	Boiling point (undersea)

THE HIGH PRESSURE at thermal vents deep under the ocean raises water's boiling point.

The World's Biggest Soup Pot

THIS IS HOW life began according to the "primordial soup" theory.

1   **BEFORE LIFE EXISTED ON EARTH,** raw ingredients—like carbon and hydrogen—sloshed together in the ocean, creating chemical reactions and making more complex molecules.

2   **A VERY, VERY LONG TIME AGO**—about 3.5 billion years—these nonliving ingredients combined to produce simple one-cell organisms like bacteria.

3   **BACTERIA GRADUALLY EVOLVED** into bigger and more complex organisms (like fish, dinosaurs, and eventually humans).

Freezing Up

Unlike almost every other substance, water expands and gets less dense when it freezes. That means ice floats, so in the winter or in cold places like the Arctic, plants and animals can survive underwater.

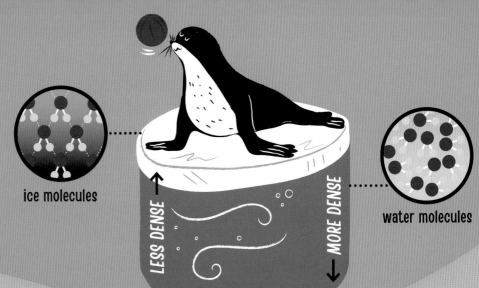

ice molecules

LESS DENSE

MORE DENSE

water molecules

Life and Water by the Numbers

8.74 MILLION = total number of species on Earth

2.2 MILLION ----> species in the ocean

6.5 MILLION ----> species on land

9% ----> estimated percentage of water species that have been discovered and cataloged

91% ----> estimated percentage of water species still unknown

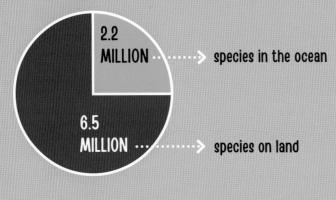

38,000
average number of different organisms in 4 cups full of seawater

17,000
number of species that live in the deep sea with no sunlight

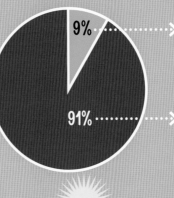

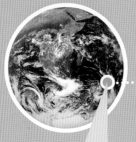

FRESHWATER ECOSYSTEMS cover less than 1% of Earth's surface, but are home to 40% of the world's fish.

2 IN 5
PEOPLE ON EARTH LIVE NEAR

AN OCEAN COASTLINE

WALKING WATER

WHEN YOU TAKE A DRINK or eat your vegetables, you probably don't think of yourself as a way for water to get from one place to another. But water is the main ingredient in our bodies. Where is all that water inside us, and what does it do?

How Much Water Is in You?

Do you know that you were born wet? As you get older, you dry out. If you arranged your family (and imaginary pet jellyfish) from wettest to driest, here's how it might look:

JELLYFISH*	BABY	1-YEAR-OLD	MAN	WOMAN	ELDERLY PERSON	OBESE PERSON
95% water	78% water	65% water	60% water	55% water	50% water	45% water

*all figures by percentage of body weight

FAT TISSUE is only about 10% water, but muscles contain 75%. So people with more fat have less water, percentage-wise, than thinner people. Men tend to have more muscle—and so more water—than women.

JUST ADD WATER

The tardigrade, or water bear, is an amazing microorganism. It can survive everywhere from the tops of mountains to the bottom of oceans, in scorching and freezing temperatures, under intense pressure, and even in outer space—unlike any other organism we know of. Why? It's because water bears have evolved an amazing ability to deal with water shortages. Their bodies, normally around 85% water, can survive without food or water for 10 years, shriveling up to only 3% water—motionless, but still alive. When they're wet again, they spring back to life.

Water in Our Bodies

63% is inside our cells

37% is around our cells

AN AVERAGE ADULT BODY contains 40 L (10 gal) of water! To drink that much water, you'd have to down one cup of water every nine minutes, 24 hours a day.

Water in Our Organs

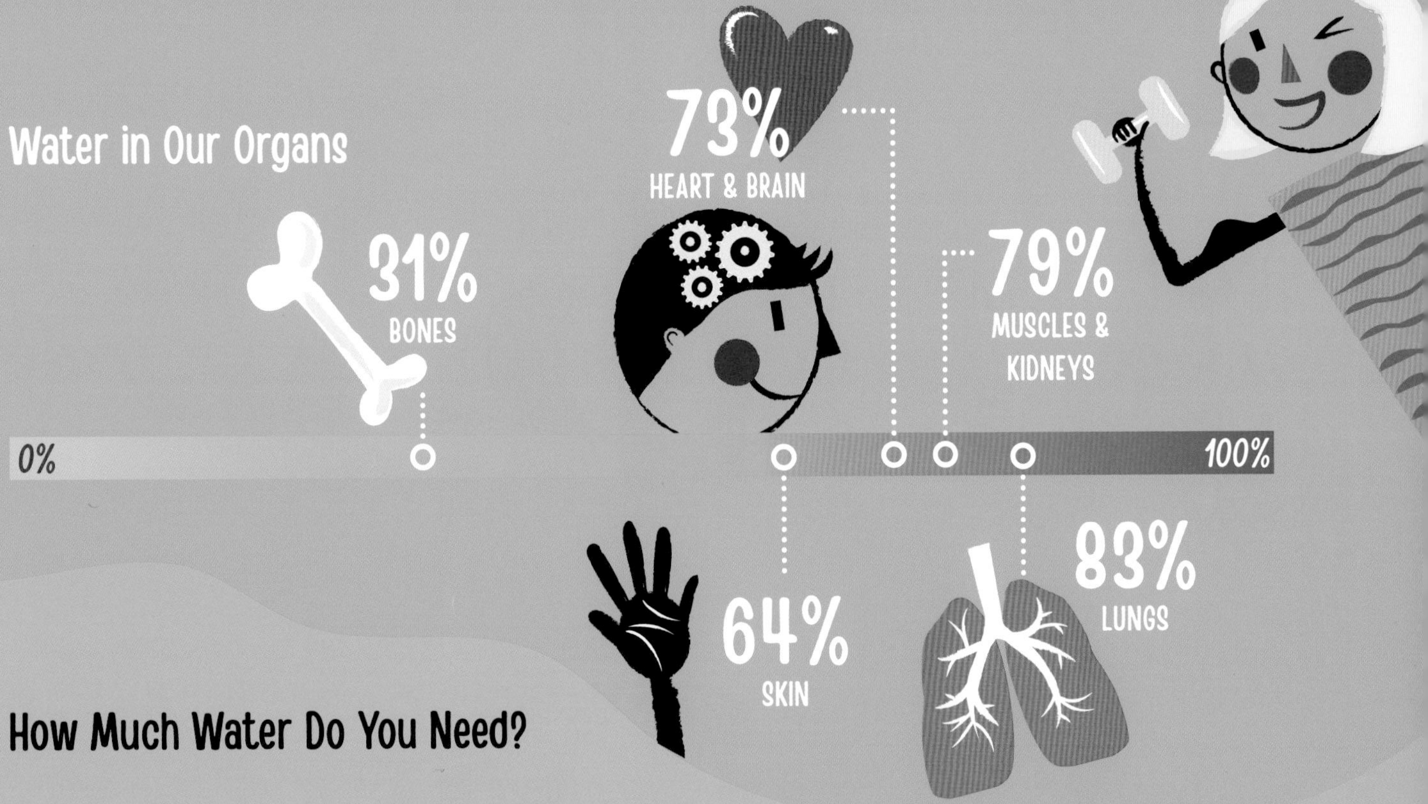

31% BONES

73% HEART & BRAIN

79% MUSCLES & KIDNEYS

64% SKIN

83% LUNGS

0% —————————————— 100%

How Much Water Do You Need?

10 CUPS

Amount of water an average 12-year-old needs per day. You need more if you're in hot weather or exercising a lot.

6 CUPS

Average amount of urine you produce per day

3 CUPS

Average amount of sweat you produce per day

20% Amount of our daily water intake that comes from food

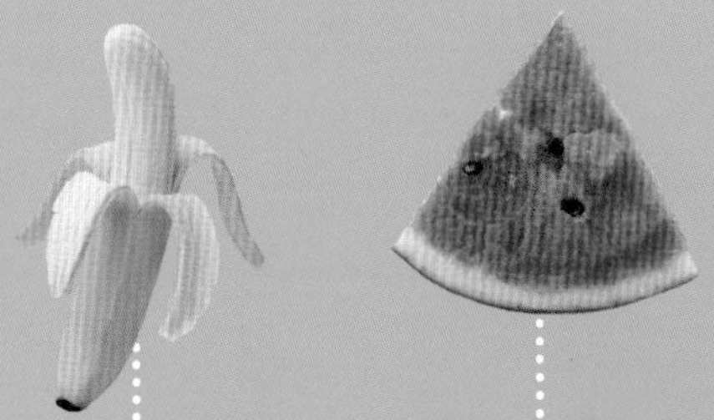

Water Content of Food

0% 3% 38% 63% 74% 84% 92% 96% 100%

HOME, WET HOME

ECOSYSTEMS are kind of like neighborhoods where different types of animals, plants, and microorganisms hang out together, interact, and often eat each other. (Okay, maybe that's not exactly like your neighborhood.) And water plays a big part in every ecosystem. From salty to fresh and flowing to still, here are some of the watery communities you'll find, and some of the creatures who live there.

SALTY

HYDRO-THERMAL VENTS
bacteria, clams, tubeworms, shrimp

CORAL REEF
coral algae, plants, fish, crustaceans, snails

BRACKISH

ESTUARY
(where rivers meet the sea)
plankton, bacteria, salmon, birds, oysters

FRESH

RIVER/STREAM
fish, insects, eels, beavers, otters

LAKE/POND
aquatic plants, algae, frogs, salamanders, freshwater fish

SALT MARSH
mussels, oysters, fish, waterfowl

MANGROVE SWAMP
mangrove trees, oysters, lobsters, shrimp, crabs

BOG/FEN
insects, frogs, cranes, woodpeckers, salamanders

MARSH
reeds, grasses, turtles, fish, herons, ducks, songbirds, hawks

SWAMP
black spruces, fish, alligators, snakes

WETLANDS

Wetlands are land that's wet—either all the time or just some of the time. There are international agreements to conserve wetlands because they support more diverse life than any other ecosystem. They also protect land from flooding, and filter pollution naturally.

THE WORLD'S BIGGEST WETLANDS

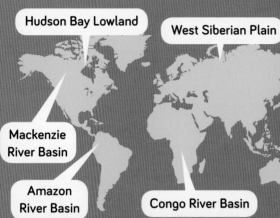

Hudson Bay Lowland

West Siberian Plain

Mackenzie River Basin

Amazon River Basin

Congo River Basin

22 OF THE WORLD'S 32 LARGEST CITIES ARE ON ESTUARIES,
INCLUDING NEW YORK CITY AND BUENOS AIRES

SOME ANIMALS CAN CHANGE

so they fit in with the water around them, whether that water is salty or fresh. This allows them to live in environments like estuaries, where salt levels in the water can change from day to day. These "osmoconformers" include squids, sharks, and rays.

BEAVERS AT YOUR SERVICE

Beavers are like a river's property managers. Their dams help create wetlands where other animals live, regulate floods and droughts, and reduce land erosion. Beaver dams have also been called the "kidneys" of the natural world because, like the kidneys in our bodies, they help filter out toxins. Silt or sand that collects near beaver dams traps harmful particles, and microbes help break them down. That makes the water down-stream of beaver dams cleaner.

1 OYSTER
CAN FILTER AS MUCH AS
4 MILK JUGS
OF WATER IN AN HOUR

OYSTERS are some of water's hardest-working residents. They feed by straining algae and particles out of water, cleaning the water in the process. Unfortunately, overharvesting in estuaries, including along the eastern US coast, has meant fewer oysters to do the job—and dirtier water.

WATER MYTHS

IN THE STORIES people have always told to explain the world, water plays a key role. In many creation myths, life comes from water. A flood of water then destroys early humans. Magical water creatures beguile us, tempt us, and sometimes save us. Finally, when we die, there are the rivers of the underworld to take us to our final resting place.

Water the Creator

YAKAMA (Washington State)

The world started out as water. The Great Chief Above was lonely, so he decided to make the world from mud, which hardened into dry land and rocks.

BABYLON

In the beginning there were two seas: the freshwater, Apsu, and the salt water, Tiamat—and a mysterious mist god, Mummu. When the fresh and salt water combined, the god of the heavens and the god of Earth and water were born.

EGYPT

Before time began, Earth was an ocean and the creator was first a cosmic serpent, and then the sun god, Ra. Ra caused the ocean to recede so he would have an island to stand on.

The Great Flood

Cultures around the world have myths or legends about a great flood. What is surprising is how similar the stories are. Here are just a few versions:

CULTURE	WHO CAUSED THE FLOOD?	WHY THE FLOOD HAPPENED
AKKADIANS (in ancient Mesopotamia, now Iraq)	The god **ENLIL**	**ENLIL WAS ANGRY** at humankind's noisy and unruly behavior.
CHINESE	**EMPEROR** of Heaven	**THE EMPEROR WAS ANGRY** at humanity's wicked ways.
GREEK	The god **ZEUS**	**ZEUS WAS ANGRY** at the arrogance of the first humans.
JEWISH/CHRISTIAN	**YAHWEH,** or God	**YAHWEH WAS ANGRY** at humans, who were sinning.
INDIAN	The god **VISHNU,** in his form as a fish	**UNKNOWN**

Introducing ... the Great Water Gods and Goddesses!

TANGAROA
Tangaroa is the Maori god of the sea and the father of many sea creatures.

ANUKET
Anuket, the Egyptian goddess of the Nile River, wore a head-dress of feathers.

SEDNA
In Inuit mythology, Sedna is the goddess of the sea and marine animals.

CHALCHIUHTLICUE
Chalchiuhtlicue is the Aztec goddess of lakes and rivers.

STORIES OF MERMAIDS OR MERMEN

come from around the world: Greece, the Philippines, Russia, China, Africa, and India, to name a few places. Mermaids are known to lure human beings with their beauty or singing, and either shipwreck or kill them.

WHO SAVED US?	HOW DID HUMANS SURVIVE?	THE HERO'S REWARD
A MAN, Utnapishtim	Ea, the god of water, visited Utnapishtim in a dream and told him to **BUILD A BOAT**.	**IMMORTALITY**
THE DRAGON YU, who grew out of the corpse of the emperor's grandson, Gun	**YU PLEADED** with the Emperor of Heaven to have mercy, so the emperor let him repair the damage.	The ruler Shun gave Yu his **THRONE.**
DEUCALION, the son of the god Prometheus	Prometheus warned Deucalion, who **BUILT A CHEST AND HID** in it with his wife.	After the flood, Zeus granted Deucalion's wish for **MORE HUMANS** to be created.
NOAH, a righteous man	Yahweh told Noah to **BUILD A BOAT** and put two of every animal on it.	Yahweh sent **A RAINBOW** as a sign of his promise never to flood Earth again.
MANU, the king of Dravida (in present-day South India)	Vishnu told Manu to **BUILD A HUGE BOAT** for his family, seven wise men, nine types of seeds, and animals to repopulate the Earth.	Manu's **FAMILY** and the seven sages repopulated Earth.

WHERE DOES THE WATER GO?

IF YOU'VE EVER had to briefly shut down the plumbing in your home for repairs, you probably realize how much you depend on having clean water at the turn of a tap. Do you ever think about how much water your house uses, and where it all goes? How about the water in your country, and all over the world?

How Can You "Use" Water, Anyway?

If water isn't ever really "used up," and keeps cycling through nature, why does it matter how much we use? Well, it's a problem when we take freshwater from a lake, river, or aquifer faster than that source can be replenished through rain and snowfall. Then we don't have water where and when we need it.

Water at Home

A North American family of four uses about 1,500 L (400 gal) of water in a single day. That's enough water to fill 10 bathtubs! What do we do with that water?

10% kitchen & drinking

30% showers & baths

20% Laundry

5% Cleaning

Drip, drip, drip ... a faucet that leaks a single drop per second wastes almost 70 bathtubs full of water per year!

The Great Shower vs. Bath Debate

Do showers really use less water than baths? It depends!
A five-minute shower using a modern, low-flow showerhead
usually uses less than an average tub filled halfway. But a longer
shower, or an older, high-pressure showerhead, can use more.

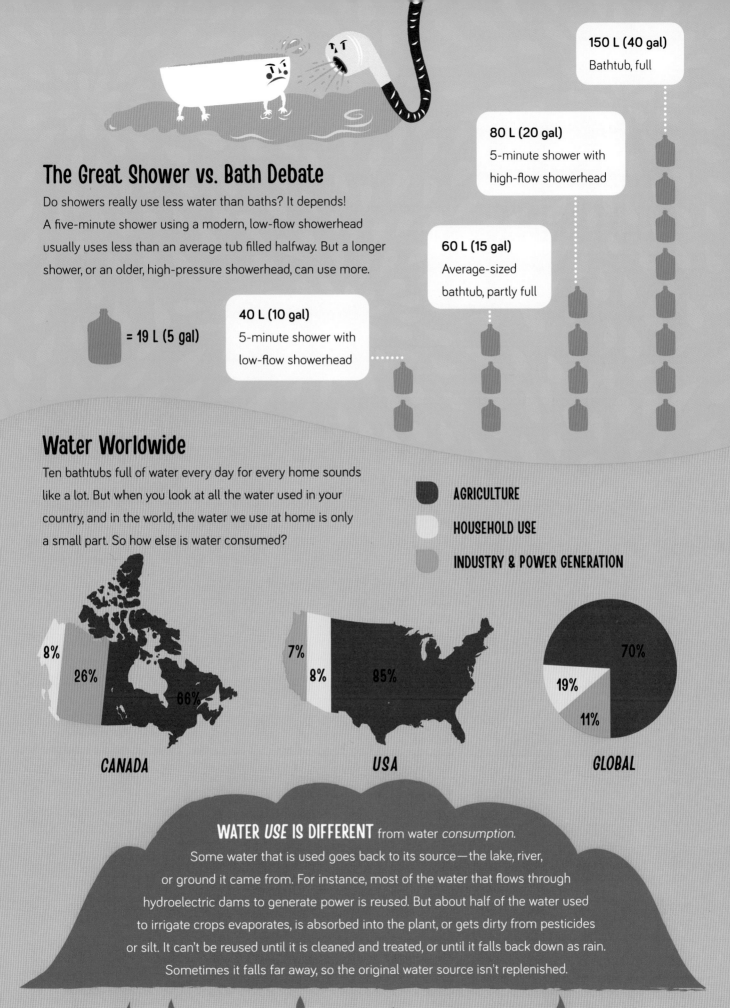

= 19 L (5 gal)

40 L (10 gal)
5-minute shower with
low-flow showerhead

60 L (15 gal)
Average-sized
bathtub, partly full

80 L (20 gal)
5-minute shower with
high-flow showerhead

150 L (40 gal)
Bathtub, full

Water Worldwide

Ten bathtubs full of water every day for every home sounds
like a lot. But when you look at all the water used in your
country, and in the world, the water we use at home is only
a small part. So how else is water consumed?

AGRICULTURE

HOUSEHOLD USE

INDUSTRY & POWER GENERATION

CANADA
8%
26%
66%

USA
7%
8%
85%

GLOBAL
70%
19%
11%

WATER *USE* IS DIFFERENT from water *consumption*.
Some water that is used goes back to its source—the lake, river,
or ground it came from. For instance, most of the water that flows through
hydroelectric dams to generate power is reused. But about half of the water used
to irrigate crops evaporates, is absorbed into the plant, or gets dirty from pesticides
or silt. It can't be reused until it is cleaned and treated, or until it falls back down as rain.
Sometimes it falls far away, so the original water source isn't replenished.

OUR WATER FOOTPRINT

WHEN YOU THINK ABOUT all the water you use in a day, you probably picture what you shower in, wash dishes with, and drink. Surprise! The water coming out of your taps is actually only *5 percent* of the total water you use! The rest is water you don't see. The measure of how much freshwater is used to make something and deliver it to you—like a pair of jeans, a cell phone, or a hamburger—is called a *water footprint.*

What Is the Water Footprint of...

Morning

a 10-minute shower
1,600 L (400 gal)

40 L (10.5 gal)
135 L (36 gal)

2,000 L (528 gal)   cotton

orange juice
170 L (201 gal)

leather
8,000 L (2,113 gal)

Midday

70 L (18.5 gal)

237 L (63 gal)

22.5 L (6 gal)

2,400 L (634 gal)

potato CHIPS

185 L (49 gal)

Evening

1 hour surfing the web   35 L (9 gallons)

50 L (13 gal)

1,260 L (330 gal)

Choco Delux

1,032 L (273 gal)

The water footprint of one hamburger is equal to 16 bath tubs!

WATER FOOTPRINTS are useful for giving you a sense of how much water goes into making things, but they don't tell the whole story. For example, something grown using mostly rainwater that goes back to its source has less of an effect on the environment than something that uses scarce surface water, or pollutes water—even if it has a lower footprint overall. Also, you get a lot more value for your water for a pair of leather sneakers that you wear for a year than for a hamburger you eat once.

The Thirstiest Countries

If you add together all the water that goes into making everything that's eaten, bought, or used by the entire population of a country, that's called a *national water footprint*. And no surprise—it's a lot! Some of that water might be used outside the country where the product is eventually consumed—for bananas grown in Central America, or a laptop made using water power in China, for instance. How do different countries stack up?

Why Are Some Feet Bigger?

THE AVERAGE PERSON IN CHINA OR INDIA doesn't use a lot of water. But because these two countries have big populations, their national water footprint is high.

PEOPLE IN THE U.S. have the biggest individual water footprints, and Canadians aren't far behind. The average North American has a high standard of living compared to the rest of the world. We eat over three times more meat than the global average and use more manufactured goods, like clothes and electronics, than many other countries.

HOT, DRY PLACES that are used as agricultural land need more water to irrigate crops because so much water is lost through evaporation.

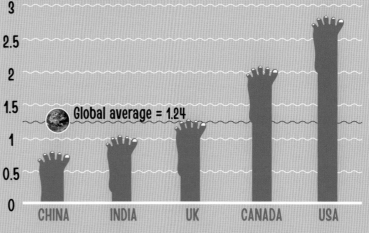

WATER FOOTPRINT PER YEAR PER PERSON
(in million L/100,000 gal)

Global average = 1.24

CHINA INDIA UK CANADA USA

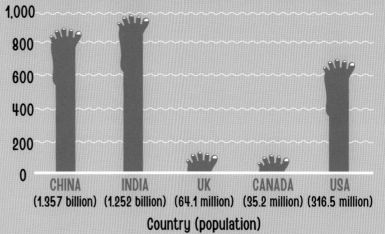

TOTAL WATER FOOTPRINT PER YEAR (in Gm³)*   Global total = 7,452 Gm³

CHINA   INDIA   UK   CANADA   USA
(1.357 billion) (1.252 billion) (64.1 million) (35.2 million) (316.5 million)
Country (population)

A cubic gigameter (Gm³) is a cube that's 1 million km (about 621,000 mi) long on each side. That's a lot of water!

THE WATER FOOTPRINT OF all the food and products that the average American consumes in a year is about 2.8 million L (740,000 gal), just over the amount of water in an Olympic-sized swimming pool.

HOLY WATER!

CAN WATER CLEAN a spot from your conscience like it cleans dirt from your hands? Symbolically, maybe it can. Water is considered sacred by religions around the world for its life-giving force as well as its purifying ability.

BUDDHISTS

sometimes meditate by imagining themselves as water, to keep their minds calm and pure. Tibetans give an offering of seven bowls of water at Buddhist shrines.

FOLLOWERS OF SHINTO

perform the ritual of Misogi, which involves washing in natural running water (especially waterfalls).

SIKHS

drop sweetened holy water on a newborn's tongue. Teenagers drink the water at baptism, symbolically taking in God's essence to live a moral life.

MUSLIMS

wash before five daily prayers to purify themselves. In Muslim countries, bathrooms often have a faucet next to the toilet for ritual cleansing. Muslims also bathe the dead.

Traditionally, **JEWS** will wash before and after meals, as well as after coming into contact with anything considered unclean.

HINDUS

use water in many ceremonies and rituals—either sprinkling it, sipping it, or washing in it. Hindu temples traditionally had large water tanks for bathing before offering prayer.

During baptism, **CHRISTIANS** sprinkle water on a baby or a new follower to clean them symbolically. When they enter church, Catholics dip their fingers in holy water.

Sacred Steam, Water, and Ice

MANY GROUPS of Indigenous North Americans purify themselves, often before a religious ceremony, in a ceremonial steam bath, or sweat lodge.

JEWISH PEOPLE pray on the shoreline to symbolically cast away their sins during the ceremony of Tashlich to begin the Jewish New Year.

DURING THE FESTIVAL of Epiphany in January, faithful Christians brave the chilly waters of an ice hole near Leningrad, Russia.

The Gods Go Swimming

Dunk! Some religions show respect to their gods by bathing them in water. During the Hindu festival of Ganesh Chaturthi, a clay image of the elephant-headed god Ganesh is submerged. Buddhist devotees bathe a statue of Buddha so that they may receive blessings.

Now That's Amazing!

MOTHER GANGES

Hindus have always believed that the water of the Ganges is pure and purifying. Scientists have discovered that its water contains viruses that destroy bacteria and kill germs, and an unusually high amount of oxygen.

FREEDOM RIVER

The River Jordan is a symbol of freedom; in the Bible, Moses and the Israelites cross it to escape slavery. Jesus was baptized in the Jordan, so Christians make pilgrimages to Israel to be baptized. Water from the Jordan has even been used to baptize royalty, including the young Prince George and Princess Charlotte of England.

29

WATER POWER!

YOU'VE PROBABLY HEARD of hydropower: a dam built on a river converts the motion of falling or flowing water into electricity. In regions where there are a lot of rivers, hydropower is the main source of electricity. But there are many other ways to get energy from water—some that might surprise you.

OCEAN THERMAL ENERGY CONVERSION (OTEC):
Water on the surface of the ocean is warmed by the Sun. Water underneath is much colder. OTEC uses that temperature difference to make energy. The warm surface water heats a gas, usually ammonia, which expands and spins a turbine (like a fan) to make electricity. Then cold water pumped from below cools it again, so the cycle can repeat. As of 2015, there is one OTEC system off the coast of Japan and several more planned in tropical waters.

TIDAL POWER:
If you've ever been caught in an undertow, you'll know that the ocean's tides are a mighty force! Energy can be generated from the power of the tides as they go in and out. A handful of tidal power stations are in use around the world, with more in development.

THE WORLD'S LARGEST HYDROPOWER DAM
is the Three Gorges Dam on China's Yangtze River. Such a huge volume of water had to be moved into the dam's reservoir when it was first completed that it slightly slowed the rotation of the Earth!

WHERE DOES THE WORLD'S ELECTRICITY COME FROM?

20% HYDRO

80% OTHER

Why Make Energy from Water?

Burning fossil fuels—oil, coal, and natural gas—creates carbon dioxide, or CO_2. CO_2 becomes trapped in the atmosphere, causing a warming effect that alters Earth's climate. So making electricity from water instead of fossil fuels can help reduce the effects of climate change. And while Earth's oil supplies will eventually run out, water won't.

OSMOTIC POWER generates energy from the difference in salt content between river water and seawater. As the river water flows into the sea, it passes through a membrane so fine that only water molecules can get by. This creates a buildup of pressure that is used to spin a turbine and produce electricity. Osmotic technology is being developed for use in Europe.

RAIN POWER: A tiny raindrop doesn't seem like it could contain much energy. But French scientists have built a device that can convert the motion energy of falling raindrops into electricity. The raindrops hit a special plastic, making it vibrate, and a generator converts the vibrations to electricity.

MICRO-HYDRO is hydropower on a small scale, using the natural flow of water to provide electricity to a home or small village. Micro-hydro systems might not look like anything more than a couple of sticks in a river. Because micro-hydro systems are easy and cheap to install, they can be used in rural areas and developing countries that might lack access to an electricity grid.

HYDROGEN: The "H" in H_2O—can be used in fuel cells that can replace oil in cars. Splitting a water atom to get hydrogen takes a lot of energy, but scientists are looking at new ways to do this using bacteria or solar power.

GEOTHERMAL ENERGY uses steam from water heated naturally inside the Earth. Wells are dug about 1.5 to 3 km (1 to 2 mi) deep to reach heat and steam underground, which can generate electricity or directly heat nearby buildings. In Iceland, over a quarter of all electricity comes from geothermal power; it's also used in most western US states.

steam   turbine   generator

hot water

WATER WHEELS, probably invented by Greeks around the third century BCE, were the first way of turning water into energy. A large wood or metal wheel spins as water pushes against buckets or blades on the outside. Traditionally, the force of the wheel spinning ground grain for flour, crushed wood or fibers to make paper or cloth, and hammered metals.

THIRSTY ENERGY

IT MIGHT NOT ALWAYS be obvious, but you need water to make energy. Sometimes a lot of it! Whenever you turn on the lights at home, use a computer, cook, or drive somewhere in a car you're using energy. You're also indirectly using the water it took to produce that energy.

Hidden Household H$_2$O

Some electricity sources use more water than others. Here's the water it takes, by source, to power an average US household for a month.*

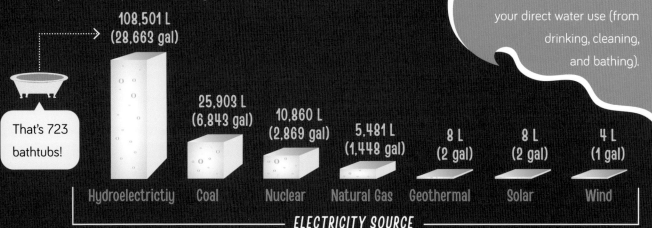

That's 723 bathtubs!

108,501 L (28,663 gal) — Hydroelectriciy

25,903 L (6,843 gal) — Coal

10,860 L (2,869 gal) — Nuclear

5,481 L (1,448 gal) — Natural Gas

8 L (2 gal) — Geothermal

8 L (2 gal) — Solar

4 L (1 gal) — Wind

ELECTRICITY SOURCE

per 1,000 kilowatt-hours of electricity

THE WATER USED TO produce electricity for your home is five times as much as your direct water use (from drinking, cleaning, and bathing).

Energy Sources in US (2014)

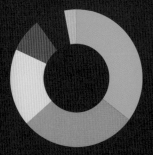

35% OIL
28% NATURAL GAS
18% COAL
8% NUCLEAR
7% OTHER RENEWABLE
3% HYDRO

TO GET OIL FROM UNDERGROUND, water is often injected into the ground, creating pressure that pushes the oil toward a well. A growing source of oil is oil sands—too sticky and thick to go in a gas tank. Water rinses sand out of the oil so it's usable.

Electricity Sources in US (2014)

39% COAL

27% NATURAL GAS

19% NUCLEAR

7% OTHER RENEWABLE

6% HYDRO

1% OIL

COAL mining can pollute rivers or fill them up with mining debris. Coal creates large amounts of CO_2 and pollution when it burns. New technologies that help to "clean" coal reduce emissions but use more water.

Renewable power sources like **WIND, GEOTHERMAL, AND SOLAR** produce electricity using very little water, and create almost no carbon emissions. Many countries, US states, and Canadian provinces are investing in more of these technologies.

HYDROELECTRICITY is renewable and has low carbon emissions. But while most water that passes through dams goes back to its source, a large amount evaporates while it sits behind dams. Dams also affect water quality and aquatic life, and change rivers and the surrounding environment. Newer, more efficient dams can reduce these effects.

Nuclear, coal, and natural gas **POWER PLANTS** use water for cooling. Some of this water evaporates, and some is returned to the lake or river it came from—but warmer than before. People might enjoy kicking back in hot tubs, but fish don't! The warm water released by power plants can be harmful to fish and create blooms of algae that disrupt the balance of nature. New technologies in power plants try to reduce water use and pollution.

NATURAL GAS is a clear gas found underground. It is used to produce electricity and to fuel some vehicles. Around half of the natural gas used in the US comes from shale rock. To release the gas from the rock, a mixture of water and chemicals is pumped underground or blasted at the rock to create cracks—a process known as hydraulic fracturing, or "fracking." But this uses a lot of water—sometimes in drought-prone areas like Texas and California—and can contaminate drinking supplies.

BIOMASS is crops like corn, soybeans, or sugar beets used to produce energy or make biofuels. This cuts down on carbon emissions from fossil fuels, but growing crops takes a lot of water and uses up a potential food source. Alternative sources of biomass, like algae or household garbage, are much more water- and energy-efficient.

WATER, ENERGY, FOOD

WHEN YOU START to think about how we use water around the world, you realize that it's only one part of a puzzle that includes two other big pieces: energy and food. The three are so tied together because each one depends on the other two. When people try to come up with ways to save water, produce more food, or use more environmentally friendly energy, they also have to think about how their ideas will affect the other parts of the puzzle.

Food crops like corn and soy can be converted to energy—biofuels—that can power cars instead of oil and gas. But growing these crops uses a lot of water, and using them for energy means they can't be used as food.

Water is used to process or refine fossil fuels like oil and natural gas, and to generate electricity.

Energy is needed to pump, treat, and transport drinking water.

Energy powers tractors and other farm machines, and is needed to transport food.

You need water to grow food or raise animals.

Growing, processing, and transporting food uses about:

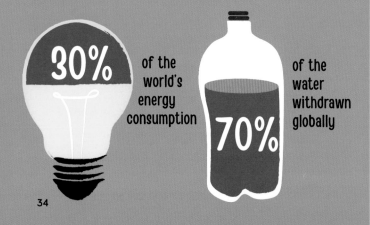

30% of the world's energy consumption

70% of the water withdrawn globally

More People, More Needs

The population of the world grows every year by about 80 million people! By 2030, it's estimated we'll need:

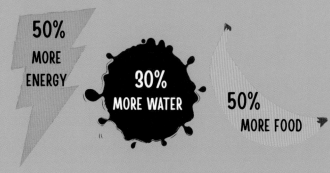

50% MORE ENERGY

30% MORE WATER

50% MORE FOOD

Growing Success

There are water-saving success stories all around the world. Here are just a few.

RICE NEEDS TO GROW in a flooded field, which means a lot of water is used. For billions of people around the world, rice is a staple food. New rice farming techniques in Vietnam create the best possible environment for the rice plant, so the yield is high while less water, seed, and herbicides are used.

IN THE DRY NORTH of Bangladesh, a very simple and inexpensive technique known as a "vegetable pool" enables people in this poor region to grow food with very little water. Seeds are planted in a bag filled with dirt, and also around the base of the bag. Water poured onto the top seeds seeps down to provide for those around the base as well.

AFTER A DEVASTATING DROUGHT from 1997 to 2009, Australia made some bold moves to protect the Murray-Darling River Basin, considered that nation's "breadbasket." They put limits on the water that farmers and others could draw from the river. Farmers now use more efficient irrigation methods, such as growing less water-thirsty crops, drip irrigation, or lining earthen ditches with concrete.

IN THE SAHEL REGION in northern Africa, low dams help to manage floodwater and enrich the soil, which reduces erosion and water loss. The water is then used for crops, animals, and forestry. The dams also help to replenish groundwater, because the water seeps into the ground as it sits, instead of rushing over it.

WATER ON THE MOVE

WHEN IT RAINS, it pours—but what if it doesn't rain again for months? Water has a frustrating habit of not always being where and when you need it. How do cities and farms survive if there's no water nearby? Fortunately, for thousands of years, people have been coming up with brilliant ideas for getting water from one place to another.

Well

What is it? A hole dug to reach groundwater, which is brought up to the surface by a pump or bucket.

First used: A 10,000-year-old stone well in Cyprus is the oldest known. It was discovered in 2009 with an ancient skeleton at the bottom!

Fact: Instead of bringing groundwater *up*, stairs can bring people *down*. Stepwells have been built in India and Pakistan for over 1,500 years, and some still exist today. The bottom of a stepwell also provides a cool place to rest on a hot day.

Canal

What is it? A human-made channel to divert water from a river or lake—either to convey ships carrying people or goods, or water for irrigation and drinking.

First used: In Mesopotamia (modern-day Iraq and Syria) around 4000 BCE, and India around 3000 BCE.

Fact: Almost 2,500 years before the Suez Canal was built, Pharaoh Necho II of Egypt tried to connect the Gulf of Suez with the Mediterranean Sea by digging a canal. It was eventually completed but later filled up with sand and wasn't used for over 1,000 years.

A *qanat* is a series of wells connected by a sloped underground tunnel. Developed by Persians around 1000 BCE, the qanat kept water cool enough to store ice from the mountains during the hot desert summer. They're still used today in many countries.

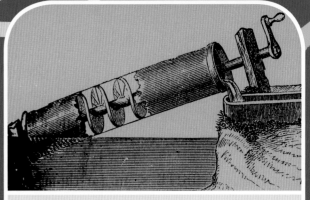

Aqueduct

What is it? In ancient times, a bridge to carry water across a valley, or over a river or stream, built on a downward slope to keep water flowing. Today, "aqueduct" can refer to any system of canals, tunnels, and pipes that carry water.

First used: Around 690 BCE, Assyrians (in present-day Iraq) built an 80-km (50-mi) stone aqueduct to carry river water from the mountains to their capital city.

Fact: There are several aqueducts in the western US. The California Aqueduct carries water over 1,120 km (700 mi) from the Sierra Nevada Mountains across the state.

Archimedes' Screw

What is it? A machine that looks like a screw inside a hollow pipe. The screw is usually turned manually, or by a windmill. The bottom part of the screw scoops up water, which moves up the spiral tube into an irrigation ditch.

First used: The Greek scientist Archimedes supposedly invented it in the third century BCE, though a version may have been used in Assyria several centuries earlier.

Fact: Archimedes probably couldn't have predicted that today we'd use his water-lifting technology for a much yummier purpose—chocolate fountains!

Water Pipe

What is it? A hollow tube used to transport water; usually part of a plumbing system.

First used: The first metal (copper) pipes, from around 2400 BCE, carried water into Egyptian temples, then drained it away into a sewer.

Fact: Lead pipes were so common before the 20th century that our word "plumbing" comes from the Latin word for "lead." Unfortunately, ingesting lead causes major health problems. Ancient Romans avoided mass poisoning because their water contained a lot of calcium, which coated the inside of the pipes.

A network of dams, canals, and aqueducts to move water across China could be the most expensive engineering project in history. By 2014, more than $79 billion had been spent on the South-to-North Water Diversion Project, and parts of it are still in the planning stages.

BEYOND THE TAP

DO YOU KNOW where your water comes from ... *before* it comes out of the tap? If you live in a city, most likely there is a giant reservoir, such as a lake, that supplies water through a vast network of underground pipes. If you live in a rural area, your water might come from a well. Either way, you can probably count on water being clean, safe, and available from your tap 24/7/365.

WHAT IF YOU LIVED IN A VILLAGE IN TANZANIA? Your water might come from a well 20 minutes or more away. Your mother or sister walks to the well at least once a day and carries back the untreated water in a barrel balanced on top of her head.

WHAT IF YOU LIVED IN THE CITY OF KARACHI, in Pakistan? The tap in your home is probably dry for much of the day. When it's not working, you get your water from a big water tank somewhere in your house, or you might buy extra water from a truck. This water might be clean, but it might not.

As of 2012:

11%

89%

About 748 million people (more than twice the population of the United States) had no access to clean drinking water.

About 6.3 billion people had clean water piped into their homes, or could get it from a nearby source (like a protected well or community tap).

WHAT IF YOU LIVED IN JEDDAH, Saudi Arabia? Your country is rich, because it has such large reserves of oil. But you are surrounded by a hot, dry desert, so water from the tap is only available one day out of nine. A lot of people buy bottled water, or water from a private water company.

Water Girls

Girls and women are in charge of collecting the household's water in many countries. That can take up to six hours a day, which makes it hard for girls and women to go to school, or grow food, or earn money. According to a study in Tanzania, if the distance to a water source is shortened from 30 to 15 minutes, girls' school attendance increases by 12%.

90% of household water in Africa is collected by girls and women.

Moving Forward

In 1990, about 1.5 million children died from diarrheal diseases, which are usually caused by contaminated drinking water or poor hygiene. By 2012 that number was down to around 600,000 thanks to improved water treatment and sanitation.

ACCORDING TO THE WORLD HEALTH

Organization, for every dollar spent on improving sanitation, there's a benefit of $5.50. That's because of less sick time for workers and less money spent treating diseases.

A 20 L (5.28 gal) container of water weighs as much as an average five-year-old. Try balancing that on your head!

GETTING TO YOU

EVER WONDER how clean water gets into our homes or how dirty water gets out? Probably not. It's easy to ignore things we can't see, like the network of pipes, tanks, motors, and cleaning facilities that make up our water systems. We only appreciate them when they *don't* work, but the fact is, humble indoor plumbing makes our modern lives possible.

How Water Gets to You

How would you feel if every time you wanted water you had to go and get it? That's what it's like in many parts of the world where people go to the village well or community tap, then carry their water home. But in developed countries like ours, pipes and pumps do the carrying for us.

1. A community's water source might be a creek, river, lake, or aquifer. Sometimes water has to travel from far away, especially in dry places.

2. Raw water is treated so it's safe to drink. Even natural spring water must be tested.

3. Reservoirs, water tanks, or towers store water.

6. Clean, treated water returns to a natural water source. If this is a river, it is often the water source for communities downstream.

5. A separate network of pipes carries our dirty water to a wastewater treatment plant.

4. Pipes buried underground carry water from the storage facility to homes and buildings. If the water has to travel uphill, pumps push it along.

In 1940, 45% of Americans lived in homes without complete indoor plumbing. By 1970, 93% of American homes had indoor plumbing, but 95% had TVs.

Distance from Major Water Source to City

Los Angeles Aqueduct
674 km (419 mi)

CAP Aqueduct
541 km (336 mi)

Colorado River Aqueduct
400 km (249 mi)

Catskill Aqueduct
190 km (120 mi)

Delaware Tunnel
137 km (85 mi)

NEW YORK CITY **LOS ANGELES** **PHOENIX**

How Far Does It Go?

Some cities are lucky to have a nearby river or lake that can supply drinking water. In other places, the water has to travel great distances through long networks of tunnels, canals, and pipes.

Dribbling Away

A surprising amount of clean, treated drinking water is wasted because it seeps into the ground through leaky pipes. This wastes not only water, but also the money and energy used to clean and move that water.

Leaky Countries

Average percentage of treated water lost by urban water systems:

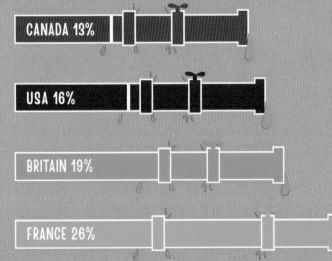

CANADA 13%

USA 16%

BRITAIN 19%

FRANCE 26%

An average North American household pays just a few dollars a day for the convenience of water piped into our homes. But that doesn't reflect its true cost. In the US, $31.6 billion is needed each year to maintain aging water systems, such as replacing old pipes and fixing water treatment plants.

IS THERE ENOUGH?

WATER, AND WHETHER WE HAVE ENOUGH of it, is a hot topic. According to the United Nations, a third of the world's people live in countries where there isn't enough clean drinking water. By 2025, this could rise to two-thirds. The good news? International programs to improve access to water, including those run by the United Nations, have already helped billions around the world.

World Water Scarcity

- enough water
- facing physical water scarcity
- facing economic water scarcity
- will face water scarcity in the future
- not estimated or not enough information available

IF YOU LIVE IN NORTH AMERICA you are lucky, because most of the continent has lots of natural sources of water. But North Americans use more water than anywhere else in the world—more than twice what Europeans use.

ALMOST TWO-THIRDS of the world's population lives in Asia, but they have just over a third of the world's water.

PHYSICAL WATER SCARCITY means there's not enough water in the area for people or living things. Hot, dry regions face scarcity, as do places where agriculture uses lots of water—like the Southwest US and the Middle East.

ECONOMIC WATER SCARCITY means there might be enough water, but people can't get to it, usually because of a lack of things like plumbing and wells. In some African countries, only 5% of freshwater—which is mostly below the surface—is used.

The Waterman of India

An organization in India, Tarun Bharat Sangh, has brought back age-old techniques for collecting rainwater—like the johad (an earthen dam) and rainwater storage tanks—to supply 1,000 villages. Since 1985, they have built over 8,600 johads and other structures. Founder Rajendra Singh was named the Stockholm Water Prize Laureate for 2015 in recognition of his extraordinary work.

So Are We Running Out?

The answer is: yes and no. There's just as much water on Earth as there's always been. So why do experts predict we could run out?

One reason is that rain doesn't fall evenly around the world. Okay. So why can't we just move the water to where it's needed? This has been done, for example in China with the South-to-North Water Diversion Project (see page 37). Unfortunately, transporting water long distances:

- is expensive;
- takes a lot of energy (to move water through long pipelines); and
- can harm the local environment and industries that depend on water, like fishing.

Another way we "run out" of freshwater is when we pollute it, or when it mixes with ocean water and becomes salty. We can't use polluted water until it has been cleaned, which can be hard to do as well as expensive.

Cold Comfort?

There's enough water in a large iceberg to supply a city of one million people for five years! So could we tow an iceberg from the Arctic to a water-scarce region, like California or the Middle East? Maybe, but there are challenges. First, it would melt on the way, like an ice cube in your drink. Second, icebergs go deep below the surface, so you'd have to leave them far offshore. People have been inventing schemes to tow icebergs since the 1800s, but so far the big technical problems haven't been overcome.

Israel gets almost half its water supply from seawater—minus the salt. About 16,000 desalination plants operate around the world, most using a process called reverse osmosis, which pushes seawater through membranes to filter out the salt. It's expensive and uses a lot of energy, but could help places facing severe drought.

WATER WARS

RIVERS AND LAKES OFTEN CROSS BORDERS, so countries, states, and provinces have to figure out ways of sharing the water they contain. If people draw water from a lake for farming, put up a dam, or pollute a river, there's less for people who live downstream. Conflict over shared water can result in signed agreements and treaties, but can also result in all-out war.

1935: National Guardsmen in Arizona patrolled the California border for a few days to protest the building of the Parker Dam on the Colorado River. Luckily, the dispute was settled in court. This was the last time an American state took up arms against another state.

PEACE

1994: An international organization was formed to manage water distribution along the Danube River in Europe. Today, 13 countries and the European Union are active members.

LATE 1800s–PRESENT: The Nile and its watershed run through 12 different countries, including Egypt, Sudan, Uganda, and Ethiopia. Since the late 1800s, countries have been negotiating ways to share the river's water rights. These agreements aren't always fair to all involved, and tensions have risen, but so far, no wars have been fought.

IN 1995, A LEADING ENVIRONMENTAL expert predicted that "the wars of the next century will be over water." However, in the last 50 years, more than twice as many treaties have been negotiated and signed than wars fought over water-related disputes.

JUNE 1967: The Six-Day War between Israel and its neighbors—Egypt, Jordan, and Syria—was partly over rights to the water in the Jordan and other rivers they shared. But even during the war, Israel and Jordan held secret talks about how to manage the Jordan River together.

2500–2350 BCE: The only war fought specifically over water happened 4,500 years ago between the neighboring cities of Umma and Lagash, located near the Tigris and Euphrates Rivers in what is now Iraq. In order to divert water to his city, the king of Umma broke down the banks on canals built by Lagash. Ultimately, though, Lagash won the war.

WAR

2009: North Korea unleashed a 4.5-m (15-ft) wall of water from its Hwanggang Dam, sending a flash flood across the border with South Korea that killed six people. It's unclear whether it was done on purpose or accidentally.

2003–PRESENT: In the Darfur region of Sudan, Africa, a civil war has killed and displaced hundreds of thousands of people. Access to water is one of the reasons for the conflict.

DIRTY WATER

BEING HUMAN IS MESSY. Not only do our bodies produce a regular supply of waste, but growing our food, running our cities, and making the things we use all create garbage and pollution, which can end up in rivers, lakes, or groundwater.

Runoff from rain or melting snow flows into rivers, and carries dirt and microbes that can make water unsafe to drink.

Factories, cars, and power plants that burn coal release sulphur dioxide and nitrogen oxide into the air. When they get together with water particles, they fall to the ground as acid rain.

When water washes dirt or oil from sidewalks, roads, and highways, it's called "urban runoff" and can end up in rivers and lakes.

Some sources of pollution are easy to recognize, like sewage coming out a pipe.

Pollution can be bigger than you think—everything from piles of plastic water bottles to stacks of tires to heaps of plastic bags.

Herbicides, fertilizers, fuel, cleaners, chemicals in cosmetics, or pharmaceuticals can pollute water.

We Love Our Coast!

Along the coastlines of New Zealand and Hawaii, volunteers have cleaned up over 1 million L (almost 280,000 gal) of garbage, thanks to the Love Your Coast project. This is only one example of how schools and children have made a difference in their local communities.

The Water Chain

When water gets polluted, the pesticide or chemical residues work their way up the food chain from plants and small animals to fish and shellfish, and then to birds and other predators, like humans, who eat fish. At each level, the pollutants become more concentrated.

In 1999, racing boat captain Charles Moore sailed through a remote part of the Pacific Ocean. To his surprise, he saw a giant pool of garbage, mostly plastics, that took a full week to sail through. There are other "garbage patches" in the ocean, but the Great Pacific Garbage Patch is the largest.

Soil washed from farm fields, construction and logging sites, or urban streets changes the natural balance of sediment in lakes and rivers. This can make it hard for water plants and animals to breathe and grow.

Tiny bacteria from animal and human waste can cause disease. Large animal farms are a major source of wastewater.

Oil transported in tankers or pipes, or from wells in the ocean, sometimes spills. While large spills are rare, they can cause devastating effects for water and the creatures who live in it.

In 2013, a lump of congealed fat and wet wipes nearly blocked the sewer system of Kingston, a suburb of London, England. The "fatberg" weighed over 15 metric tons, and was about the size of a bus.

CLEAN UP!

CHEMICALS, MICROBES, human and animal waste: there are lots of things that can make water too dirty for people to drink and use. So it's a good thing we've figured out many ways to clean up after ourselves. Of course, the best way to deal with water pollution is to create less of it, or none at all.

The Gross Factor

Treating dirty water (yes, that icky sludge we'd rather not think about) is serious business. Our dirty water goes through several stages of cleaning before it can be reused:

- Big things that can be easily collected, such as garbage, leaves, or branches, are removed.

- The sewage flows into large tanks and sits so that heavy stuff can settle to the bottom, and grease, oil, and other floating things can be skimmed off the top.

- Good microbes are mixed with the sewage water to clean the water of organics, such as sugars, fats, and carbon. That's right—bugs clean our water.

- Many different methods are used for the final stage of treatment, including sand filters, more microbes, and disinfection.

Some of the waste removed from sewage can be reused for other purposes, like fertilizing plants.

settling tanks

sewage treatment plant

sewage water pipes

In 1854, Doctor John Snow proved that an outbreak of cholera in London was a result of untreated sewage contaminating the local water supply. Since then, our understanding of how water cleanliness affects health has grown. Better water sanitation is one of the main reasons people live longer now than they did in the past, though access to clean water is still a challenge in many parts of the world.

P2, not P-U!

Pollution prevention, or P2, means reducing pollution so there's less to clean up. Here are some P2 ways to keep water healthy.

Farmers can use many different methods to reduce runoff and keep the soil in their fields. Even something as simple as planting trees, like the ones around this creek in Iowa, reduces the amount of silt in the water. Farmers can also reduce the amount of pesticides that end up in water by planting crops in rotation, using pest-repelling plants, or encouraging beneficial bugs that eat pests.

Good urban planning in cities and towns can reduce the amount of dirty water in local water sources, and ensure wastewater is treated before it's released back to its natural source.

What You Can Do to P2

- ✔ If you live near an ocean, river, or lake, you can join in, or organize, a beach cleanup.

- ✔ To keep garbage out of the water, recycle your paper, glass, cans, and plastics, and compost food scraps.

- ✔ Be aware of the drain! Storm drains are meant for water, not garbage. Put your trash in the can.

- ✔ Avoid toiletries with microbeads—tiny bits of plastic found in some skin scrubs and toothpastes. Microbeads don't biodegrade and are too small to be filtered out, so they end up in water sources, where fish can eat them. Check labels for "poly" ingredients, like polyethylene (PE), polypropylene (PP), or polymethyl methacrylate (PMMA).

Your Garbage Is My Gold

Another way to think about pollution is that it's simply waste. When we reduce waste, more raw materials are being put to good use, and we don't have to spend as much money cleaning up after ourselves.

At the "eco-industrial park" in Kalundborg, Denmark, nine businesses share materials and waste, so one company's waste becomes another's raw materials. For instance, extra steam produced by a power plant is sent to an oil company to use in refining, and the oil refinery's wastewater is pumped to the power plant for cleaning. This saves freshwater and reduces waste and heat pollution.

You can apply the eco-industrial concept in your home by using bathwater to keep the lawn green, or giving your food scraps to your neighbor to compost for their garden.

WATER WISE

IT FLOWS in pipes under our streets and floats in clouds in the sky. It moves through our bodies, keeping us alive, and it's the secret ingredient in the food we eat and energy we use. Water's not exactly invisible, but like many things that matter most, it's very easy to take for granted.

After reading this book, you might start to notice water a little more. You might think about where it comes from, what you put into it, and how the things you do every day affect it. Here are a few ways to start doing that.

Discover Your Water

✓ Where did it come from before it got to your tap? Some cities, states, and provinces have websites that tell you where your water supply originates and the steps it goes through to make it clean.

✓ Do you live near beaches, rivers, or wetlands? Are there issues like dams, pollution, or farming that affect the water in your area? You could join a group dedicated to keeping your local water source healthy, or even start one yourself.

Every Drop Counts

✓ Even simple things like turning the tap off when you're brushing your teeth, or cutting a minute off your regular shower time, saves water.

✓ Think up creative ways to reduce and reuse water at home. The ice cubes from the bottom of your drink could go on the houseplant. Wash fruits and veggies in a pan of water instead of running the tap.

✓ Can you do a job with less water, or none at all? Sweep the sidewalk rather than hosing it down, or wash the car with a bucket and sponge.

✓ Go on leak patrol—even little leaks add up! In one year, a leaky faucet that drips once per second wastes enough water to take more than 180 showers. A showerhead leaking 10 drops per minute wastes enough to wash 60 dishwasher loads.

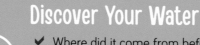

OFFICIAL LEAK PATROL

Chill Out!

- There are lots of good reasons to cut back on our carbon emissions and fight climate change, and protecting our water is a big one. Anything you can do to save energy and reduce waste is good for the planet and for water, too. And in turn, it's good for you.

- Walking and biking on short trips is excellent exercise and cuts down on carbon emissions from cars. Eating more plants and less meat and dairy uses less energy and water, and produces less carbon. Buying, using, and reusing only what we need cuts down on the energy used to make and ship things.

Worldwide Water

- Learn about water access issues around the world. Kids in many countries can't depend on having clean, healthy water.

- If you want to help, find an international organization or water project you can support. You could get your class or school to fundraise so that a village can build a well or rainwater catchment. Many organizations will send you pictures and updates as the project progresses, so you can see the results of your contribution.

- Get your friends together and pledge to go two weeks without drinking anything but tap water, then donate the money you would have spent on other drinks to a water charity. You can also help by sharing information online and writing emails to politicians to support global water security.

Keep It Clean

- Our sewage systems work really hard! Help them out by flushing only toilet paper, not wet wipes, tissues, sanitary products, or garbage.

- Say no to polys and save the fish! Look on cosmetic labels for plastic microbeads. You can also support petitions and laws to ban microbeads.

aquifer: an underground layer of rock, sand, or gravel that contains water. Unconfined aquifers have water flowing in from the surface while confined aquifers are trapped between layers of rock.

atmosphere: the envelope of gases surrounding a planet

atmospheric water: water vapor found in the air and in clouds

bog: a type of *wetland* consisting mostly of spongy peat (decaying plant matter) and moss. Bogs are common in the eastern part of North America, as well as in northern Europe and Russia, and are fed by rainfall.

cubic gigameter: a unit of measurement equaling the volume of a cube that's 1 billion meters (1 million kilometers, or around 621,000 miles) on each side

cubic kilometer: a unit of measurement equaling the volume of a cube that's 1 kilometer long on each side. A cubic kilometer of water is almost 1 trillion liters (264 billion gallons).

cubic mile: a unit of measurement equaling the volume of a cube that's 1 mile long on each side. A cubic mile of water is over 4.1 trillion liters (1 trillion gallons).

eco-industrial park: a network of businesses that cooperate with each other to reduce waste and share resources

economic water scarcity: a situation in which a source of water exists, but people lack the means to access or use it—for instance, in places where there are no pipes or wells to supply clean water

ecosystem: a community of living things and their environment (including air, water, and soil), which interact as a system

El Niño: a climate pattern caused by a band of unusually warm Pacific Ocean water, which causes changes in air pressure, global temperatures, and rainfall

estuary: the area where a river or stream meets the ocean

evaporation: the process through which a liquid changes to a gas—for example, when water is heated and becomes vapor

evapotranspiration: the process through which water is transferred—through both *evaporation* and plant *transpiration*—from Earth's surface to the atmosphere

fen: a type of peat-containing *wetland* similar to a *bog* but less acidic because it's fed by groundwater

fossil fuels: underground deposits of dead plant and animal matter that have decayed over hundreds of millions of years, which can be extracted and burned to generate energy. Oil (petroleum), coal, and natural gas are types of fossil fuels.

groundwater: water found beneath Earth's surface—in the soil or in spaces between rock. A usable amount of groundwater is called an *aquifer*.

hydrothermal vent: a crack in the planet's surface through which super-hot water from inside the planet flows. Hot springs and geysers are types of hydrothermal vents found on land; other vents are found deep undersea.

hydrous minerals: minerals, or rock, containing water in their molecular structure. Under pressure deep in the Earth, water molecules are squished and fused into the molecules of the surrounding rock.

irrigation: artificial watering of land to grow food. There are many methods of irrigation, including pipes, sprinklers, ditches, and stream diversion.

mangrove swamp: a type of coastal *wetland* found in tropical regions, consisting mostly of mangrove trees, which can survive in both salt and freshwater

microbeads: tiny plastic spheres used in some cosmetics, including skin scrubs and toothpastes. Because microbeads don't break down in water and are too small to filter out, they create water pollution and can be consumed by fish.

microorganism: a living thing that's too small to see without a microscope. Bacteria, fungi, algae, and protozoa are types of microorganisms. *Microbe* usually refers to a disease-causing microorganism.

organism: any living thing, including animals, plants, and microorganisms

osmoconformer: a water-dwelling animal that can adapt its body to the surrounding environment, so it can survive in either salt or freshwater. Starfish, mussels, lobsters, jellyfish, skates, and sharks are osmoconformers.

physical water scarcity: a situation in which there is not enough water to supply people who live in a particular area. It happens in places where there is not enough natural water supply (like in the desert) or where the water supply is overused (like on agricultural land).

primordial: something that exists from the beginning of time, or is very ancient

P2 (pollution prevention): an environmental concept that focuses on preventing waste and using fewer things that cause pollution rather than on cleaning up after pollution has already been created

reservoir: a lake, usually human-made, used to collect and keep water for human use

salt marsh: a type of muddy coastal *wetland* that's flooded by salt water from the ocean

sanitation: the provision of clean water and sewage disposal

surface water: water found on the surface of the planet, including oceans, lakes, rivers, and wetlands

tardigrade: a microscopic water-dwelling animal with eight legs, also called a water bear

tidal bore: a natural phenomenon that happens when a wave from the ocean travels up a river or bay against the direction of the current. They usually occur in just a few places around the world, but can cause dangerous surges of turbulent water.

transpiration: the process by which plants absorb water through their roots, then release it as water vapor through tiny holes in their leaves

urban runoff: excess water from rain storms or melting that flows from cities (because it can't be absorbed through surfaces such as concrete) into lakes, rivers, and bays. This runoff can carry pollutants—such as motor oil, trash, or lawn fertilizers—along with it.

water access: a measure of how many people in a community can obtain an adequate supply of safe drinking water within a convenient distance of where they live

water consumption: the amount of water used for a given task that isn't returned to its source; for instance, the water used to irrigate crops that is absorbed by the plant, or becomes contaminated with pesticides or silt

water footprint: the total amount of freshwater consumed to produce and deliver a product. A person's water footprint is calculated by adding up all the water they use directly as well as the water it takes to produce the food, energy, and goods they use or consume.

watershed: an area of land that's connected because all the water on or under it goes to the same place—for instance, all the land surrounding a river

water system: a network of pipes, canals, or other human-made constructions designed to provide water for people to use

water use: the amount of water used for a given task. Water use may not equal *water consumption,* because some water used is returned to its source. For example, some of the water used by hydroelectric plants flows back into the river it came from, so it's not consumed.

wetland: land that's wet either all the time or in some seasons. Swamps, bogs, marshes, and mangrove swamps are types of wetlands.

SELECTED SOURCES

Introducing the Amazing ... Water!
supercritical fluid, "What Is a Supercritical Fluid?" Budapest University of Technology and Economics website, sfe.kkft.bme.hu/en/current-research.html.

hydrous minerals, Charles Fishman, *The Big Thirst: The Secret Life and Turbulent Future of Water* (New York: Simon and Schuster, 2011), 32–34.

estimated water amounts, ocean and hydrous minerals, "How Much Water Is in the Ocean?" National Ocean Service website, oceanservice.noaa.gov/facts/oceanwater.html; Andrew Williams, "Scientists Detect Evidence of 'Ocean's Worth' of Water in Earth's Mantle," Astrobiology Magazine, Aug. 21, 2014, www.astrobio.net/news-exclusive/scientists-detect-evidence-oceans-worth-water-earths-mantle/.

Wet Planet
Orion Molecular Cloud Complex, "Discovery of Water Vapor Near Orion Nebula Suggests Possible Origin of H20 in Solar System," *Harvard University Gazette*, Apr. 23, 1998, news.harvard.edu/gazette/1998/04.23/DiscoverofWater.html.

age of water on Earth, Elizabeth Gibney, "Earth Has Water Older than the Sun," *Nature*, Sept. 26, 2014, nature.com/news/earth-has-water-older-than-the-sun-1.16011.

theories of how water came to Earth, Andrew Fazekas, "Mystery of Earth's Water Origin Solved," *National Geographic* online, Oct. 30, 2014, news.nationalgeographic.com/news/2014/10/141030-starstruck-earth-water-origin-vesta-science/; Brian Greene, "How Did Water Come to Earth?" *Smithsonian Magazine* online, May 2013, smithsonianmag.com/science-nature/how-did-water-come-to-earth-72037248/?no-ist.

Where on Earth Is the Water?
volume of water on Earth, "How Much Water Is There on Earth?" *Deskarati*, deskarati.com/2011/07/30/how-much-water-is-there-on-earth/.

percentages of salt water and freshwater on Earth, Peter H. Gleick, ed., *Water in Crisis: A Guide to the World's Fresh Water Resources* (Oxford: Oxford University Press, 1993), 13.

breakdown of surface water sources, The USGS Water Science School, "The World's Water," U.S. Geological Survey website, water.usgs.gov/edu/earthwherewater.html.

Extreme Water
Lake Vostok, "Lake Vostok Breakthrough: Russian Scientists Drill 'Clean' Hole into Antarctic Subglacial Basin," *Russian Times* online, Jan. 25, 2015, rt.com/news/226127-lake-vostok-russia-water/.

Nile, Encyclopaedia Britannica Online, s.v. "Nile River," britannica.com/place/Nile-River.

Mt. Waialeale, Encyclopaedia Britannica Online, s.v. "Mount Waialeale," britannica.com/place/Mount-Waialeale.

Iquique, The USGS Water Science School, "Rain and Precipitation," U.S. Geological Survey website, water.usgs.gov/edu/earthrain.html.

Black Sea Undersea River, Richard Gray, "Undersea River Discovered Flowing on Sea Bed," *The Telegraph* online, Aug. 1, 2010, telegraph.co.uk/news/earth/environment/7920006/Undersea-river-discovered-flowing-on-sea-bed.html.

Lake Baikal, Alroy Menezes, "Lake Baikal, World's Largest Freshwater Body, Turning Into A Swamp, Ecologists Say," *International Business Times*, Sept. 9, 2014, ibtimes.com/lake-baikal-worlds-largest-freshwater-body-turning-swamp-ecologists-say-1682512.

Qiantang River tidal bore, Karin Muller, "Tsunami-Like River Tides Are Surfing's New Frontier," *National Geographic News*, Feb. 22, 2005, news.nationalgeographic.com/news/2005/02/0222_050222_tidalbore_2.html.

Lake Turkana, "Lake Turkana National Parks," UNESCO website, whc.unesco.org/en/list/801.

Water's Amazing Journey
2 minutes of evaporation; 1 football field, Fishman, *The Big Thirst*, 35.

33 percent of drinking water, The USGS Water Science School, "Groundwater Use in the United States," U.S. Geological Survey website, water.usgs.gov/edu/wugw.html.

2 months of showers, The USGS Water Science School, "Rain and Precipitation," U.S. Geological Survey website, water.usgs.gov/edu/earthrain.html.

cloud lifespan, Bob Swanson, "Answers: Clouds, Fog, Rain, Snow, Drizzle," *USA Today*, Apr. 15, 2007, usatoday30.usatoday.com/weather/resources/askjack/archives-clouds-precip.htm.

evaporation from groundwater, S.M. Tanvir Hassan, "Assessment of Groundwater Evaporation Through Groundwater Model with Spatio-temporally Variable Fluxes," International Institute for Geo-Information Science and Earth Observation website, Mar. 2008, itc.nl/library/papers_2008/msc/wrem/tanvir.pdf.

aquifers, The USGS Water Science School, "Aquifers," U.S. Geological Survey website, water.usgs.gov/edu/earthgwaquifer.html.

Water, Weather, and Climate
most information from "Ocean Explorer," NOAA website, oceanexplorer.noaa.gov/facts/climate.html; Earth System Research Laboratory, "Water and Climate," NOAA website, esrl.noaa.gov/research/themes/water/.

climate change and water, United States Environmental Protection Agency, "Water Resources," EPA website, epa.gov/climatechange/impacts-adaptation/water.html.

Dry Times
drought, National Drought Mitigation Center, "Types of Drought," drought.unl.edu/DroughtBasics/TypesofDrought.aspx.

Atacama, Hillary Mayell, "Ancient Chile Migration Mystery Tied to Drought," *National Geographic News,* Oct. 24, 2002, news.nationalgeographic.com/news/2002/10/1024_021024_ChileAtacama.html.

Mozambique, US Agency for International Development, "USAID/OFDA Success Story—Mitigating Drought and Cyclone Effects in Mozambique," Reliefweb, Oct. 21, 2009, reliefweb.int/report/mozambique/usaidofda-success-story-mitigating-drought-and-cyclone-effects-mozambique.

The Soup of Life
primordial soup theory, "How Life Evolved: 10 Steps to the First Cells," *New Scientist* online, Oct. 14, 2009, newscientist.com/article/dn17987-how-life-evolved-10-steps-to-the-first-cells/; Peter Tyson, "Life's Little Essential," *Nova,* PBS website, Jan. 4, 2004, pbs.org/wgbh/nova/evolution/liquid-of-life.html.

life and water by the numbers, Tim Wall, "8.74 Million Species on Earth," *Discovery News,* Aug. 23, 2011, news.discovery.com/earth/plants/874-million-species-on-earth-110823.htm; "How Many Species on Earth? About 8.7 Million, New Estimate Says," *Science Daily,* Aug. 24, 2011, sciencedaily.com/releases/2011/08/110823180459.htm.

number of people who live by an ocean coastline, "Human Settlements on the Coast," UN Atlas of the Oceans, oceansatlas.org/servlet/tstatus=ND0xODc3JjY9ZW4mMzM9KiYzNz1rb3M~.

Walking Water
how much water is in … , The USGS Water Science School, "The Water in You," U.S. Geological Survey website, water.usgs.gov/edu/propertyyou.html.

water in food, University of Kentucky College of Agriculture, "Water Content of Fruits and Vegetables," www2.ca.uky.edu/enri/pubs/enri129.pdf.

Home, Wet Home
water ecosystems, University of California Museum of Paleontology, "The Freshwater Biome," ucmp.berkeley.edu/exhibits/biomes/freshwater.php; Defenders of Wildlife, "Types of Wetlands," defenders.org/wetlands/types-wetlands; North Carolina Water Quality Program, "Types of Wetlands and their Roles in the Watershed," North Carolina State University website, water.ncsu.edu/watershedss/info/wetlands/types3.html.

cities on estuaries, NOAA Ocean Service Education, "Estuaries," National Oceanic and Atmospheric Administration website, oceanservice.noaa.gov/education/tutorial_estuaries/welcome.html.

beavers, "About Beavers," Beavers: Wetlands & Wildlife (website), beaversww.org/beavers-and-wetlands/about-beavers/.

oysters, "Oyster Reef Habitats," Smithsonian Marine Station at Fort Pierce, sms.si.edu/irlspec/Oyster_reef.htm.

tardigrade, William Herkewitz, "Secrets of the Water Bear, the Only Animal That Can Survive in Space," *Popular Mechanics* online, Aug. 7, 2014, popularmechanics.com/space/a11137/secrets-of-the-water-bear-the-only-animal-that-can-survive-in-space-17069978/.

Water Myths
Babylonian and Egyptian creation myths, Philip Wilkinson and Neil Philip, *Visual Reference Guides: Mythology* (New York: Metro Books/DK Books, 2007), 141, 226–27.

Yakima creation myth, Michael McKenzie et al., *Mythologies of the World: The Illustrated Guide to Mythological Beliefs & Customs* (New York: Checkmark Books, 2001), 17.

great flood, Wilkinson and Philip, *Visual Reference Guides: Mythology;* and *National Geographic: Essential Visual History of World Mythology* (Washington, DC: National Geographic, 2008).

Where Does the Water Go?
water use in the home, Stephen Leahy, *Your Water Footprint: The Shocking Facts About How Much Water We Use to Make Everyday Products* (Toronto: Firefly Books, 2014), unpaginated. Figures vary, depending on the source.

water worldwide, "Water Consumed this Year," Worldometers, worldometers.info/water/; AQUASTAT website, Food and Agriculture Organization of the United Nations (FAO), 2015, fao.org/nr/water/aquastat/main/index.stm. Accessed Mar. 3, 2015.

water use and water consumption, Paul Reig, "What's the Difference Between Water Use and Water Consumption?" World Resources Institute, wri.org/blog/2013/03/what's-difference-between-water-use-and-water-consumption; Brian Richter, "To Understand Water, Learn the Math," *National Geographic* online, Mar. 28, 2014, voices.nationalgeographic.com/2014/03/28/to-understand-water-learn-the-math/.

Our Water Footprint
water footprints, water footprints by country, A.Y. Hoekstra and A.K. Chapagain, "Water Footprints of Nations: Water Use by People as a Function of Their Consumption Pattern," in *Water Resource Management* (2006): 40, 42; see also waterfootprint.org/Reports/Hoekstra-2008-WaterfootprintFood.pdf, 54.

Note to readers: The statistics in this book are drawn from the latest information available at press time. In cases where numbers may vary, averages have been used. Unless otherwise noted, all online sources were last consulted August 2015.

Holy Water!

amrit and Sikhism, "Amrit Ceremony," BBC website, bbc.co.uk/religion/ religions/sikhism/ritesrituals/amrit.shtml.

misogi and Shintoism, "Purification: Wand or Waterfall," The Pluralism Project, Harvard University, pluralism.org/religion/shinto/purification; John D., "Misogi and Cold Water," Green Shinto (website), Oct. 24, 2013, greenshinto. com/wp/2013/10/24/misogi-and-cold-water/.

Ganesh Chaturthi, Encyclopaedia Britannica Online, s.v. "Ganesh Chaturthi," britannica.com/topic/Ganesh-Chaturthi.

Jordan River, Daniela Ralph, "Low-key Christening for Prince George," *BBC News* online, Oct. 23, 2013, bbc.com/news/uk-24627323; bbc.com/news/ magazine-33382957.

Water Power!

most information on this spread from Sarah Zielinski, "Seven Unexpected Ways We Can Get Energy From Water," Smithsonian.com, Sept. 5, 2014, smithsonianmag.com/science/seven-unexpected-ways-we-can-get-energy- water-180952625/?no-ist.

rain power, Amarendra Swarup, "Plastic Converts Raindrops to Electricity," *Physics World* online, Jan. 29, 2008, physicsworld.com/cws/article/ news/2008/jan/29/plastic-converts-raindrops-to-electricity.

Thirsty Energy

water used to produce electricity, Wendy Wilson, Travis Leipzig, and Bevan Griffiths-Sattenspiel, "Burning Our Rivers: The Water Footprint of Electricity," River Network, Apr. 2012, climateandcapitalism.com/wp-content/uploads/ sites/2/2012/06/Burning-Our-Water.pdf.

energy sources in the US, U.S. Energy Information Administration, "U.S. Energy Facts Explained," EIA website, eia.gov/energyexplained/index. cfm?page=us_energy_home; Nick Cunningham, "How Much Water Does the Energy Sector Use?" Oilprice.com, Apr. 13, 2015, oilprice.com/Energy/ Energy-General/How-Much-Water-Does-The-Energy-Sector-Use.html.

electricity sources in the US, U.S. Energy Information Administration, "Frequently Asked Questions," EIA website, eia.gov/tools/faqs/faq. cfm?id=427&t=3.

water-energy nexus, Richard W. Healy, William M. Alley, Mark A. Engle, Peter B. McMahon, and Jerad D. Bales, "The Water–Energy Nexus—An Earth Science Perspective," U.S. Geological Survey Circular 1407, 2015, pubs.usgs. gov/circ/1407/pdf/circ1407.pdf.

Water, Energy, Food

water, energy, food nexus, "Water, Food and Energy Nexus," UN-Water, unwater.org/topics/water-food-and-energy-nexus/en/.

vegetable pools, Agriwaterpedia, s.v. "Vegetable Pool—Bangladesh," agriwaterpedia.info/wiki/Vegetable_pool_-_Bangladesh.

Sahel, Agriwaterpedia, s.v. "Water Spreading Weirs—Sahel," agriwaterpedia. info/wiki/Water_spreading_weirs_-_Sahel.

rice farming techniques in Vietnam, Dr. Georg Deichert, Nina Seib, and Le Thi Nguyet Thu, "Promoting Green Growth, Food Security and Healthy Ecosystems in the Vietnamese Mekong Delta with the System of Rice Intensification (SRI)," *Agriwaterpedia,* agriwaterpedia.info/images/a/aa/ GIZ_%282011%29_Promoting_Green_Growth%2C_food_security_and_ healthy_ecosystems_in_the_Vietnamese_Mekong_Delta_with_SRI.pdf.

Murray River, Brian Richter, "The Australian Approach to Water Crisis: Work With Farmers," *National Geographic* online, June 5, 2014, voices. nationalgeographic.com/2014/06/05/the-australian-approach-to-water- crisis-work-with-farmers/.

Water on the Move

skeleton found in well, "Stone Age Wells Found in Cyprus," *BBC News* online, June 25, 2009, news.bbc.co.uk/2/hi/europe/8118318.stm.

stepwells, Rima Hooja, "Channeling Nature: Hydraulics, Traditional Knowledge Systems, And Water Resource Management in India: A Historical Perspective" (book proposal), Infinity Foundation website, infinityfoundation. com/hooja_book.htm.

early water pipes, Christopher Jones, "More Inventions of the Ancient Near East," Gates of Nineveh (blog), May 10, 2012, gatesofnineveh.wordpress. com/2012/05/10/more-inventions-of-the-ancient-near-east/.

Beyond the Tap

water access in Pakistan, David Hebert, "Impossible Odds, Irrepressible Hope: Pakistan's water woes and the science that can solve them," *Earth* online, Oct. 5, 2010, earthmagazine.org/article/impossible-odds- irrepressible-hope-pakistans-water-woes-and-science-can-solve-them.

water access in Tanzania, water girls, "Water and Gender Factsheet," UN-Water, Oct. 5, 2013, unwater.org/publications/publications-detail/ en/c/204289/.

access to drinking water, World Health Organization and UNICEF, "Progress on Drinking Water and Sanitation: 2014 Update," unwater.org/fileadmin/ user_upload/unwater_new/docs/jmp.2014_eng.pdf.

WHO and improving sanitation, World Health Organization, "Sanitation" (factsheet), June 2015, who.int/mediacentre/factsheets/fs392/en/.

"Moving Forward" figures, World Health Organization, "Water Supply, Sanitation, and Hygiene Development," who.int/water_sanitation_health/ hygiene/en/.

Getting to You

water supply system, "Drinking Water Distribution Systems," United States Environmental Protection Agency, water.epa.gov/lawsregs/rulesregs/sdwa/tcr/distributionsystems.cfm.

indoor plumbing in the US, Fishman, *The Big Thirst,* 109.

leaky countries, Fishman, *The Big Thirst,* 5; *Britain,* Andrew Johnson and James Burton, "Water Torture: 3,300,000,000 litres are lost every single day through leakage," *The Independent* online, Jul. 25, 2010, independent.co.uk/news/uk/home-news/water-torture-3300000000-litres-are-lost-every-single-day-through-leakage-2034999.html; *Canada,* Environment Canada, "2011 Municipal Water Use Report," Government of Canada, 2011, ec.gc.ca/Publications/B77CE4D0-80D4-4FEB-AFFA-0201BE6FB37B%5C2011-Municipal-Water-Use-Report-2009-Stats_Eng.pdf.

cost to maintain water systems in US, from "Drinking Water" and "Wastewater" *2013 Report Card for America's Infrastucture,* American Society of Civil Engineers, 22 and 43.

Is There Enough?

water scarcity facts and map, World Water Assessment Programme (WWAP), *World Water Development Report 4,* Mar. 2012, accessed from UN–Water website, un.org/waterforlifedecade/scarcity.shtml; *Facts and Figures from the United Nations World Water Development Report 4,* zaragoza.es/contenidos/medioambiente/onu/789-eng-ed4-res12.pdf.

Waterman of India, "The Water Man of India Wins 2015 Stockholm Water Prize," Stockholm International Water Institute website, Mar. 20, 2015, siwi.org/prizes/stockholmwaterprize/laureates/2015-2/; "Our Mission," Tarun Bharat Sangh website, tarunbharatsangh.in/our-mission/.

water from icebergs, Marshall Brain, "What if People Wanted to Use Icebergs as a Source of Fresh Water?" Howstuffworks, science.howstuffworks.com/environmental/earth/oceanography/icebergs-as-water.htm.

desalination, David Talbot, "Desalination out of Desperation," *MIT Technology Review,* Dec. 16, 2014, technologyreview.com/featuredstory/533446/desalination-out-of-desperation/.

Water Wars

most information on this spread from Alex Prud'homme, *The Ripple Effect: The Fate of Freshwater in the Twenty-First Century* (New York: Scribner, 2012), 196–99.

future conflicts, John Vidal, "How Water Raises the Political Temperature Between Countries," *The Guardian* online, June 25, 2010, theguardian.com/environment/2010/jun/25/river-water-disputes-tension-shortages.

Dirty Water

sources of water pollution, C. Michael Hogan, "Water Pollution, *The Encyclopedia of Earth,* Nov. 17, 2014, eoearth.org/view/article/156920/.

Love Your Coast project, loveyourcoast.org.

Great Pacific Garbage Patch, National Geographic Education, "Great Pacific Garbage Patch," education.nationalgeographic.com/education/encyclopedia/great-pacific-garbage-patch/?ar_a=1.

Clean Up!

P2, "Pollution Prevention," Environment Canada website, http://www.ec.gc.ca/p2/.

Kalundborg eco-industrial park, "The Green Industrial Municipality," City of Kalundborg website, kalundborg.dk/Erhverv/The_Green_Industrial_Municipality.aspx; Ellen MacArthur Foundation, "Kalundborg Symbiosis," ellenmacarthurfoundation.org/case_studies/kalundborg-symbiosis.

fatberg, "UK's Biggest 'Fatberg' Discovered in London Sewer," Thames Water website, Jul. 30, 2013, thameswater.co.uk/media/press-releases/17205.htm.

Water Wise!

many suggestions and figures from United States Environmental Protection Agency, "Water Sense—Fix a Leak Week," EPA website, epa.gov/WaterSense/pubs/fixleak.html.

FURTHER READING

Leahy, Stephen. *Your Water Footprint: The Shocking Facts About How Much Water We Use to Make Everyday Products.* Toronto: Firefly Books, 2014.

Mulder, Michelle. *Every Last Drop: Bringing Clean Water Home* (Orca Footprints). Victoria: Orca Book Publishers, 2014.

Strauss, Rochelle. *One Well: The Story of Water on Earth.* Toronto: Kids Can Press, 2007.

Woodward, John. *Water* (Eyewitness Books). London: DK Publishing, 2009.

INDEX

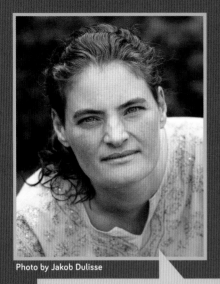

Photo by Jakob Dulisse

Photo by Shaker Paleja

Photo by Ben Macleod

Between them, **Antonia Banyard** and **Paula Ayer** have written three previous books for young readers. This is their first book together. Antonia lives in Nelson, British Columbia, and Paula lives in Vancouver.

Belle Wuthrich is an illustrator and designer who lives in Vancouver, British Columbia.

PHOTO CREDITS